Perception

A PHILOSOPHICAL SYMPOSIUM

Perception

A PHILOSOPHICAL SYMPOSIUM

Edited by
F. N. SIBLEY

METHUEN & CO LTD
11 NEW FETTER LANE LONDON EC4

First published 1971
by Methuen & Co Ltd
11 New Fetter Lane London EC4
© 1971 Methuen & Co Ltd
Printed in Great Britain by
Northumberland Press Ltd, Gateshead

SBN 416 65900 4

Distributed in the USA
by Barnes & Noble Inc

Contents

Contents

Preface

The symposium papers in this volume were presented at a Colloquium on Perception organized by the Philosophy Department of the University of Lancaster and held on 10-12 April 1970.

Some of the papers have undergone revision prior to publication, but they are substantially as presented at the Colloquium.

F. N. SIBLEY
Lancaster, November 1970

On What is Seen

I

G. J. WARNOCK

If a person A wants something X, and X is P, does it follow that A wants P? One is inclined to say not: for if Smith wants to eat that oyster, and that oyster is poisonous, one might not wish to say that Smith wants to eat something poisonous. There are in fact cases where one does make a move of this sort: for example, faced with the problem of getting food and harmless fluids into a confirmed alcoholic, one might well say 'The trouble is that he only wants things that are bad for him' – i.e. he only wants alcohol, and alcohol is bad for him. However, it seems one can say that, where 'A wants X' is true, one does not *always* get an unexceptionable truth by replacing 'X' with something else that X is, by some other expression that is true of X. In this respect the notion of seeing seems more straightforward than the notion of wanting; for in this case it seems perfectly all right to say in general that if A sees X, and X is P, then A sees P – if Smith sees the picture over my fireplace, and that picture is the most valuable object in my house, then Smith sees the most valuable object in my house. If asked to explain *why* this works in general, I suppose one should say that the truth or falsehood of 'A sees X' is quite independent of the question how, or even whether, A himself is able, or prepared, or inclined to specify, or identify, or describe what he sees – so that, if it is true that he sees X, we can obtain, without any further reference to him or his views, further truths, by replacing 'X' with any expressions at all that are in fact true of X: whereas, with wanting X, it may be that sometimes at any rate we have to consider, not just what X is, or what is actually true of X, but in what light, so to speak, A himself envisages X in wanting it. A's seeing X, in fact, has nothing

1

to do with what he knows or thinks or is inclined to say, if anything, *about X*; so that, just as, if *A* kicks *X*, he therein kicks whatever *X* is, so he sees whatever *X* is, if he sees *X*.

However, unfortunately (though I suppose not surprisingly), recognizing cases in which, for seeing, this sort of uninhibited substitution is truth-preserving is not just a matter of looking out for the appropriate verbal pattern – that is, the pattern '*A* sees *X*; and *X* is *P*; so *A* sees *P*'. There are at least two ways in which this verbal pattern can be treacherous – it may, in a nutshell, incorporate either the wrong sort of 'is', or the wrong sort of '*P*'. I am not at all sure, as will doubtless emerge, quite what is the proper way to describe what goes wrong in such cases, but I think one can say in a preliminary sort of way that, when one gets this verbal pattern, sometimes the 'is' is not an 'is' of identity, and sometimes, more complicatedly, the '*P*' is such as, so to speak, to re-act back on the verb, or, perhaps better, to modify the sense of the sentence as a whole. I hope to diminish in due course the obscurity of that remark.

First, about the 'is'. I want to consider here briefly a kind of case which Austin mentions in *Sense and Sensibilia*, but of which his treatment there is somewhat wavering. There is a passage (pp. 87 ff.) in which he is arguing against the idea of 'different senses' of 'see': and in particular he says that, from the fact that the question 'What does *A* see?' may frequently have a number of different, but all alike true, answers, it does not follow that more than one sense of 'see' is involved. At least one point that he has in mind here is the one just mentioned – namely that, if *A* sees *X*, then – leaving the '*A* sees ...' exordium untouched and unaffected – we can put in *salva veritate*, for '*X*', anything that *X* is. Just as, if that piece of painted wood is Jones's front door, and I kick that piece of painted wood, then – in no different sense of 'kick' – I kick Jones's front door, so, if that man is the vice-chancellor and I see that man, then – in no different sense of 'see' – I see the vice-chancellor. What we have here is nothing like different senses of 'see', but different ways of specifying, or identifying, the thing seen – ways that, if all correct, are intersubstitutable *salva veritate*.

There is, however, one particular sort of case, which Austin has in mind here, to which he appears inclined to apply this principle, although he recognizes that actually the case is in some ways different (pp. 82 ff.). *A* sees a tiny, silvery speck of light in the night sky: *A* sees a star many times larger than the earth. There is, of course, a case in which both these things would be true. Does *A* see these things in different senses of 'see'? Austin says not, perfectly correctly in my view. But why not? Well, as Austin says, in such a case it would be wholly natural to say that the tiny, silvery speck *is* a star many times larger than the earth – cp. that piece of painted wood *is* Jones's front door, that man *is* the vice-chancellor: and if *A* sees the speck, he therein sees what (i.e. that which) the speck is. However, as Dretske has recently observed, and indeed as Austin himself observes, at least by implication, in a footnote, the cases are not quite alike. For in the cases of the piece of wood and the man, we have genuine identities; whereas it seems we have to say that, in the case of the star, we do not. If that man is the vice-chancellor, then it not only follows that, if I see that man, I see the vice-chancellor, but also that, if I sit next to that man at dinner, I sit next to the vice-chancellor, and so on; whereas, as Austin observes, if that white dot on the horizon is a house, and I live in that house, it does not follow that I live in a white dot; nor could I advertise a white dot, though I might advertise my house, for sale in the pages of *Country Life;* and when, as we continue our walk, the white dot grows larger, my house does not grow larger; and so on.

It does not follow from this, I think, that anything Austin says in this connection is wrong, but only that, for what he says, he does not fully work out the right reason, and even seems, by implication, inclined to rely on the wrong one. If *A* sees a tiny, silvery speck in the night sky, and that speck – as it is certainly natural to say – is an enormous star, then it does indeed follow that he sees the star; and I can see no reason for supposing that there is more than one sense of 'see' involved here. But in virtue of what does it follow? Well, in virtue of the fact that the speck *is* a star. Yes; but what sort of observation is that? As we have just noted, it seems not to be construable as saying that X is Y in the way that implies that what is true of X is true of Y and vice versa; and if so, it can't be for *that*

3

reason that, if *A* sees *X*, then *A* sees *Y* – as when, if I kick that piece of wood, I kick Jones's front door. So how is the 'is', in 'That speck is a star', to be construed?

Well, as Austin observes in his footnote, where we can say naturally enough 'That speck in the sky is a star', we cannot comfortably put it the other way round – though it may hold in general that, if *A* is *B*, then *B* is *A*, in this case there is something markedly peculiar about the sentence 'That star is a speck'. Why is this peculiar? One is inclined to say here, and I think rightly inclined, to say that this is not an *identity* – though in some appropriate sense that speck may be a star, it is simply not true of that star, not just like that, that *it is* a speck; 'a speck' surely is not, just like that, something that it could simply be said to *be*, as it might be, for example, the celestial object first observed in 1829. It is not that the star simply *is* a speck, but rather that a speck is what it visually *appears as*, when looked at in these conditions, with the naked eye, here and now. One may observe, consistently with this, that there is, in fact, something peculiar about 'That star is a speck' only if one omits to think of that sentence as occurring in an appropriate setting, a setting that makes clear how it is to be taken. Taken all on its own, the sentence seems simply to say what the star *is*; but how, one then asks, could *that* be what it is? The words, however, might in fact very naturally be said, and taken, simply as a comment on the way the star *appears* – as when, having taken a close look from our space capsule at that enormous star, I say later, struck for instance by the speed at which we must have been travelling away from it, 'Look, that enormous star is a speck'. It follows, then, that, if I see the speck, I see the star, *not* because the speck is what the star is, nor (in a sense) because a star is what the speck is, but because a speck is what, now and from here, the star visually appears as: and, of course, if I see what *X* visually appears as, I see *X*. Austin was right, then, in holding that '*A* sees a tiny speck in the sky: that tiny speck is a star: therefore, *A* sees a star' is a valid argument, but was wrong in suggesting, as *ex silentio* he seems inclined to do, that it is valid for just the same reason as '*A* sat next to that man at dinner: that man is the vice-chancellor: therefore, *A* sat next to the vice-chancellor'. The 'is' in the former argument, though it indeed makes the argument valid, is not the same 'is' as the 'is' in the latter one; and the arguments are not actually the same, though they are both valid and the form of their wording is identical.

One further comment. If, as suggested, the 'is' in 'That speck is a star', though not a straightforward identity 'is', happens to be such as to make this argument-form valid, one might wonder whether there are other non-straightforward 'is's that would make it invalid. I am sure the answer is that there are, but have not been able to think up a very convincing example. But here is a rather unsatisfactory one. Suppose that there is something of which it might be unobjectionably said 'That is the vice-chancellor', and suppose that I have seen that thing. Does it follow, from that information alone, that I have seen the vice-chancellor? I suggest that it does not. For perhaps the thing that I have seen is a bust of the vice-chancellor; and although it is certainly unobjectionable for many purposes to say of a bust (picture, etc.) that it *is* what it could also be said to be *of*, it seems plain enough that *this* sort of 'is' is not such as to permit the inference in question. That is the vice-chancellor (in a sense); and I have seen that; but perhaps I have never seen the vice-chancellor. In this case, unlike the case of the speck and the star, the sense of the 'is', as emerges from its literal-minded expansion, is clearly *not* such as to carry the implication that one who sees this, sees what this is.

I can bring up my next question by way of considering another, very cryptic paragraph of Austin's, which occurs later in the same passage in *Sense and Sensibilia* (pp. 98-9). Consider the sentences 'I saw a man shaved in Oxford' and 'I saw a man born in Jerusalem'. As Austin rightly says, there might be a single piece of seeing by me, of which both of these sentences might be uttered with perfect truth; e.g. Smith, who was born in Jerusalem, is being shaved in a barber's shop in Oxford, and I watch that operation, so that I both see a man born in Jerusalem, and also see that man shaved in Oxford. However, there is, perhaps in more than one sense, something funny about this. Austin, who is still arguing against 'different senses' of 'see', ends his brief paragraph with the remark that 'if there *is* ambiguity here, it is not the word "saw" that is

5

ambiguous', thereby seeming to hint that there may well be ambiguity somewhere. Perhaps we should look for it.

Well, the fact is, I think, that – whether or not 'saw' may be ambiguous here, as I don't think it is – both these *sentences* are certainly ambiguous, though in this case it seems natural to take one in one way, and the other in the other. In this case, 'I saw a man shaved in Oxford' seems naturally to be taken as meaning that I saw him *being* shaved in Oxford, I witnessed the operation; but no doubt the words could also be taken as meaning that I saw a man, not being shaved, but who had previously *been* shaved, in Oxford. For example, 'You may think Cambridge barbers are pretty good, but for sheer perfection of finish you should see a man shaved in Oxford'. By contrast, 'I saw a man born in Jerusalem' is naturally taken here as meaning that I saw a man who previously was, or had been, born in Jerusalem; but the words, I suppose, could conceivably be taken differently, as meaning that I saw a man *being* born in Jerusalem – though less naturally so, partly perhaps because one doesn't usually expect people to be witnesses of births, and partly because one would expect babies to be seen being born, rather than men. In any case, here there certainly is ambiguity. In one sense, for instance, to see a man shaved in Oxford one must be in – or at least within visual range of – Oxford, but in the other sense not. In the other sense, I might of course quite well see in Cambridge a man shaved in Oxford.

But now let us go back, with these sentences before us, to the question we were previously considering – the question, that is, of the validity of the argument-form '*A* sees *X*; and *X* is *P*; so *A* sees *P*'. Does this work in such cases as these? It seems to me that Austin implies, again *ex silentio*, that it does – it is not that he explicitly says so, but then he does include this paragraph, without explicit disclaimer, in a discussion the general tenor of which is certainly to the effect that this argument-form is generally a valid one.

Well, in view of the ambiguity we have just noticed, we have, of course, two cases to consider. Picking the sentence 'I saw a man born in Jerusalem', let us first take this to mean, as it most naturally would, that I saw a man who was, or had been, born in Jerusalem, or of whom that he was born in Jerusalem is true. Our question then is: does 'I saw a man born in Jerusalem' *follow* from the premises that I saw that man, and that that man was born in Jerusalem? The answer, I suggest, is that it clearly does. I saw Smith: Smith was born in Jerusalem: therefore, I saw a man born in Jerusalem, i.e. of whom that he was born in Jerusalem is true. Similarly, if I were to say that I had never seen a man shaved in Oxford, you might cogently prove to me that (in this sense) I had, by saying: 'But you saw Smith, didn't you? Well, Smith was shaved in Oxford; so actually you *have* seen a man shaved in Oxford.' The reason why this argument is a good one, of course, is that, for it to be true that (in this sense) I saw a man shaved in Oxford, or born in Jerusalem, all that is required is that I should have seen a certain man, and that of that man it was actually true that he was shaved in Oxford, or born in Jerusalem. There does not come into it any question, for example, as to what I may have known or believed or been inclined to say, if anything, about the man that I saw; what matters is what is true about that man.

But what if we take the words in the other sense? If we take 'I saw a man shaved in Oxford' to mean, as it might, that I saw him *being* shaved in Oxford, does *this* follow from the premises that I saw that man, and that that man was being shaved in Oxford? I suggest that it does *not* follow; but here we must be careful not to give the wrong reason for its not doing so. Having said, I think rightly so far as it went, that the argument worked, for the other sense, for the reason that in that sense no question arose as to what I may have known or believed or been inclined to say, if anything, about the man that I saw, one might be tempted to say that it does not work for this sense because, in this sense, such questions do arise – that, for instance, it is not enough that it should simply be true of the man that I saw that he was being shaved in Oxford, for the question arises whether I *knew* that to be true. But that would be wrong. That would be to confuse 'I saw a man being shaved in Oxford' with 'I saw that a man was being shaved in Oxford'. 'I saw that a man was being shaved in Oxford' does indeed require for its truth, not only (indeed, not

7

necessarily) that I saw that man, and that it was true that that man was being shaved in Oxford, but also that (rather roughly) I thereby came to *know* that he was being shaved in Oxford: for, though he was being shaved in Oxford and I saw him, I did not see that he was being shaved in Oxford if I did not know that he was – if, for instance, I did not recognize as shaving the operation that was going on when I saw him. But that I saw him being shaved does not require this apprehension on my part; it requires indeed that he was being shaved, but not that I knew or noticed or realized that he was, Similarly, observing a man whom I perhaps take to be a visitor going into your house and leaving again with a suitcase, I see – as I may afterwards discover – a malefactor making off with all your silver; I do not see *that* he is committing that burglarious act, since I do not realize that he is, but I do in fact see him committing it, as I may afterwards learn.

But if that is so, why does 'I saw a man being shaved in Oxford' *not* follow from the facts that he was being shaved in Oxford, and that I saw him? What is required, I think, is some further condition, not indeed about what I knew or noticed or realized, but about *what I saw*. Suppose that I see, through a rather narrow window, the back of your head and neck and perhaps your shoulders, but that I cannot see anything that is going on in the room in front of you, for instance no movement of any sort. In that case, I see you (enough of you, let us assume, to count simply as seeing you); but, even if it happens to be true that you are at that moment being shaved, it seems to me not true that I see you being shaved. I do not see any such thing going on. Somewhat similarly, if I see you, a barely visible dot on the other side of the valley, too far away for me to distinguish, for instance, your limbs, then I do not, I think, see you scratching your head, even if, when I see you, you *are* scratching your head. To put generally the point that such examples suggest, one might say that, if I am to see you doing or undergoing some action or process X, then at least something that counts as or partly constitutes doing or undergoing X must actually be discriminable – though *not* necessarily recognized or noticed – *in* what I see; it is not enough that I merely see what is *in fact* doing or undergoing that action or

8

process. But if that is so, then, while if I see you and you are being shaved in Oxford, I would *usually* therein see you being shaved in Oxford, it does not straight off *follow* that I do; for it needs also to be true, as no doubt it usually would be, that I see – even if I do not recognize as such – at least some of the goings-on in which your being shaved consists.

But now, if *that* is so, then I think we can venture to say – though with due trepidation in face of experts on these matters – that the words 'I saw a man shaved in Oxford', and others of that pattern, are not merely ambiguous, but grammatically ambiguous. Austin, I think, was perfectly right in saying that it is not the word 'saw' (particularly) that is ambiguous; but the sentence as a whole is, I think, taken in one sense, grammatically different from the same words taken in the other sense. I do not really know how to put this point with professional polish, but an amateurish account of the matter might go thus. If we take 'I saw a man shaved in Oxford' to mean that I saw a man *who was* shaved in Oxford, of whom that he was shaved in Oxford is true, then the object of the verb 'saw' is 'a man'; and the words 'shaved in Oxford' serve to 'qualify' that object, i.e. simply to add something *about* the thing designated by the grammatical object 'a man'. That being so, then the truth-conditions of the sentence are simply that the man be seen by the designated subject, and that what is said of him in the qualifying words should be true of him. But if we take 'I saw a man shaved in Oxford' to mean that I saw a man *being* shaved in Oxford, then it seems to me that there is reason to say that the object of the verb 'saw' is no longer just 'a man', but rather the whole phrase 'a man being shaved in Oxford' – that phrase being paraphrasable, not as 'a man *who was* being shaved in Oxford', but rather as 'the shaving of a man in Oxford'. That is, speaking ontologically, on this reading what is seen is not an object, but an event – not a man to whom something is happening, but rather the happening of something to a man. And in that case, of course, the truth-conditions would be, as we have found they are, rather different; for, of course, seeing something happening to an object is a different matter from (even if, as seems plausible, it must include) just seeing the object, and even from just seeing

9

the object of which it is then true that that thing is happening to it. If this is right, then Austin seems to have been right about 'see'; for it seems that the ambiguity of the sentences he considers resides in the words, specifically in the *grammar* of the words, that appear as *object* of the verb 'see', and no case appears for the supposition that 'see' is itself ambiguous, or at any rate ambiguous here.

Incidentally, it seems not to be merely sentences of the somewhat truncated, compressed kind that Austin cites that are thus ambiguous – ambiguous in that, being compressed, they admit of verbally and grammatically different expansions. There are, I think, un-truncated forms that may also be ambiguous. The sentence 'I saw him crossing the room' would, I think, naturally be taken as having as object the happening-expression (if I may call it so) 'him crossing the room', i.e. the crossing of the room by him. But consider the sentence 'I saw him thinking about natural deduction'. This sentence, if it gets by at all, could scarcely be taken in the same way; for though thinking about natural deduction is, I suppose, a process or happening, it is presumably not a process or happening that could be seen – it has no *visible* constituents. Thus, I think, we would have to take these words grammatically differently, notwithstanding their identity of verbal form – as, not 'I saw (the process of) him thinking about natural deduction', but 'I saw him, *and* (or perhaps, when) he was thinking about natural deduction'. As a matter of fact one would, I think, in such a case be likely to signal explicitly that the latter way is the way the words should be taken – in writing by, for instance, putting in a comma after 'I saw him', or by some correspondingly slight variation, a pause for instance, in speaking. In 'I saw him at his desk, thinking about natural deduction' it is really quite clear that thinking about natural deduction is to be construed, not as what I saw an instance of, but simply as what he was doing *when* I saw *him*.

My conclusions, then, are not at all surprising, though I think – and even, in a sense, hope – that they have not always been recognized. (1) In general it is, I suggest, perfectly valid to argue: '*A* sees *X*; *X* is *P*; so *A* sees *P*'. Since *A*'s own characterizations (or whatever) of *X*, if any, have nothing to do with his *seeing* X (though they might have something to do with, for instance, his *wanting* X), we can always in such a case replace '*X*', *salva veritate*, with any designations that are actually of the same thing. However, caution is called for here, since (2) it is, as I fear it is rather strikingly unoriginal to say, not in general the case that 'is' is unambiguous; when we have '*X* is *P*', it is not always the case that '*X*' and '*P*' are therein offered as designations of the same thing. For instance (3), with particular relevance to the present topic, we do *not* have such a case where visual objects such as specks, blurs, dots, etc., are said to *be* physical objects like stars, aeroplanes, houses, etc. Thus (4) '*A* sees that speck: that speck is a star: so *A* sees a star' is, though valid, *not* an instance of the valid argument-form in (1) above: it is not, that is, valid for *that* reason. Next (5), it is sometimes necessary also to be cautious about grammar. In '*A* sees *X*; *X* is *P*; so *A* sees *P*', let '*X*' be 'a man', and '*P*' be 'a man shaved in Oxford'. In that case, the argument is valid only if its conclusion is read, rather unnaturally, simply as containing a certain characterization of the *X*, i.e. the man, that *A* sees. If it is not so read, the thing breaks down; for even if *A* sees a man, and that man is (being) shaved in Oxford, it does not *follow*, though no doubt it would usually be true, that he sees (the happening of) a man being shaved in Oxford. To put it generally (6), if we start with '*A* sees *X*', and go on to say truly that *X* is *P*, we can validly conclude that *A* sees *P* only if '*P*' is such as to leave the grammar of the conclusion the same as that of the first premise. If I see a man, and that man is scratching his head, it does not follow that I see a man scratching his head: for 'a man scratching his head', in the putative conclusion, is not a person-designating direct object of the verb 'see', as 'a man' is in the premise that I see a man. I am actually by no means confident that that is the right way of putting the point that is involved here; but the point, in *some* form, looks right to me, however exactly it ought to be put.

II

D. M. TAYLOR

I have a nasty feeling, commenting on Warnock's paper, that in seizing what I take to be the bull by the horns I may in fact be grappling with quite a different species of animal. This I shall doubtless discover.

Warnock begins by comparing wanting with kicking. He maintains that while inferences of the form 'A wants X and X is P, so A wants P' are not always unexceptionable, inferences of the form 'A sees X and X is P, so A sees P' are, like those involving kicking, relatively straightforward. Cases that appear difficult may be separated as being really of a different form.

In his first paragraph Warnock puts his goods fairly and squarely on the table. He says:

> ... the truth or falsehood of 'A sees X' is quite independent of the question how, or even whether, A himself is able, or prepared, or inclined to specify, or identify, or describe what he sees – so that, if it is true that he sees X, we can obtain, without any further reference to him or his views, further truths, by replacing 'X' with any expressions at all that are in fact true of X ...

and, later in the paragraph,

> A's seeing X, in fact, has nothing to do with what he knows or thinks or is inclined to say, if anything, *about* X; so that ... he sees whatever X is, if he sees X.

There are two distinct theses in these remarks.

(1) What A sees, or whether A sees X, has nothing to do with what A knows or thinks or is inclined to say about what he sees, or about X.

(2) If A sees X and X is P, A sees P.

Warnock appears to think that the fact that (2) is true is explained by the truth of (1); I am not sure what logical relationship he believes to hold between (1) and (2), possibly

13

entailment. It is, however, arguable that (2) entails something like (1).

I wish to argue that (1) is false and hence cannot explain (2). However, I believe (2) to be largely true; hence the possibility that (2) entails (1) must be examined and rejected.

It does not seem absurd to suggest that (2) entails (1). For if it is the case that if A sees X and X (unknown to A) is a P then A (unknown to him) sees a P, might it not be true of everything that A sees that he neither knows nor conceives it to be the case that he sees those things?

Objections

1. It may be that for any true description, 'T', of something, X, seen by A, A sees a T (possibly without thinking what he sees is a T). It does not follow that for any possible description, 'D', of X, A might see X and not think he sees a D. It might be a necessary condition of A's seeing anything that he believed or thought what he saw to be something, D, either truly or falsely.

2. Indeed it might be a necessary condition of A's seeing something, X, that he thought or believed at least one true thing about X; the inference pattern, 'If A sees X and X is P, A sees P' would still hold, for one can only begin making such inferences on the premise that A sees something and that premise could involve this condition. If A loves Mabel and Mabel is a princess, A loves a princess. But it would not follow that A might love Mabel without thinking or believing anything true about her.

To take an example from seeing. Suppose A must see a colour, if he sees. A cannot see a colour, C, and not be aware of it, for how *could* he see C and not be aware of it?

(i) Suppose he sees X and $X = C$ (though he is unaware of this); then X must be a colour, in fact it must be C, or $X \# C$.

(ii) Suppose instead he sees X, which has the colour C, though he is unaware of the colour of X; in this case he sees a CX but does not see C, i.e. he does not see a colour.

It will nevertheless still be true that, *if A sees C and C is P,*

A sees P, e.g. where 'C'='red' and 'P'='the colour most women like on their lips'.

There are in fact two versions of Warnock's (1):
(1a) A might see something, X (say, a princess), and not think or know anything about X (*the princess*).
(1b) A might see something, X, and not think or know anything about *what he sees*.

It seems to me that the distinction between (1a) and (1b) is important in only two possible cases, (i) if thinking is purely intentional and (ii) if a thought about an appearance of a thing one sees is not a thought about that thing.

(i) Is the inference 'A thinks something, X, about what he sees and what he sees is a princess, so A thinks something, X, about a, or that, princess' satisfactory? It seems to me that it is. I might think a man I saw an ill-mannered fellow, and only later discover that I had thought the Prime Minister an ill-mannered fellow. Once one has identified a material object of thought, 'thinking' behaves just like 'seeing'.

(ii) Suppose one thinks something, X, about what one sees, Y, where Y is the appearance of something, Z, and where one's seeing Y constitutes one's seeing Z. One sees Y and Y is Z, so one sees Z. Does it follow that one thinks X about Z? It seems to me that at least on some occasions it does. I see a grey spoon-shape, which is what a cat appears to me as (though I am unaware of this). I think, 'That's a pretty shape'. It follows that, given what I see is a cat, my thought is a thought about *that* cat (though not about cats).

I conclude, doubtless rashly, that there is no need to distinguish Warnock's (1a) from his (1b).

I want now to turn to an examination of Warnock's thesis (1). The force of this thesis seems to me to be as follows. Given I see anything, the question what I see is to be settled by asking what is in fact before me (in my field of vision). When I think I see something that is not before me, either
  (i) I see something else and take it for what it is not, or
  (ii) I take myself to be seeing something when I am not.

Objections

I shall begin by arguing that seeing is in fact more like wanting and thinking than kicking.

There appear to be two ways of talking about seeing, wanting and thinking, and correspondingly two kinds of object of the verbs 'see', 'want' and 'think'. We may contrast

$T(a)$ I'm thinking about a triple-glazed window

with

$T(b)$ I'm thinking about a, or some particular, or that triple-glazed window.

No one would suggest that unless something like $T(b)$ were true, $T(a)$ could not be. Similarly we may contrast

$S(a)$ I see a cottage nestling amongst green hills, or I see a floating red patch or patch of red

with

$S(b)$ I see a, or that, or some particular cottage...etc., or I see a, or that, or some particular floating...etc.

I see no reason for denying that $S(a)$ might be true while $S(b)$ is false.

The difference between the (a)-statements and the (b)-statements in both cases (and in corresponding cases for wanting) comes out clearly in the applicability or otherwise of the question 'Which one?' This question is always applicable to objects of kicking, but not always to objects of these other three verbs. There is perhaps more of a problem about the objects of vision than about objects of thought in (a)-statements. I am not too clear what Miss Anscombe[1] meant when she compared intentional objects with direct objects. But I take it that her point is that where the question 'What are you Q-ing, or Q-ing about?' does not receive an answer to which the question 'Which one?' is appropriate, one should not think that the object of the Q-ing falls into a special class. A doctor talking about a tuberculosis-prone man, though about no man in particular, is not talking about a special kind of tuberculosis-prone man. (If this were so, the sentence I have just uttered would be the beginning of a regress.)

If I am asked what I was thinking *about*, what I shall say is something that forms part of what I say when I report what

16

I was thinking, e.g. 'A triple-glazed window', which is part of 'A triple-glazed window must be a splendid insulator'. I identify what I was thinking by uttering a sentence, what I was thinking *about* by uttering a part of that sentence. If I am then asked what 'A triple-glazed window' refers to, my reply must be that if the question is about the *kind* of object referred to, the answer is, again, a triple-glazed window; whereas if the purpose is to discover *which particular* object was intended, the answer is that none was.

Similarly, if I am asked what I see, I suppose I might try painting a picture, i.e. I might try to identify what I see by 'uttering' a picture.

When someone describes what he sees or is thinking about, we may attempt to identify a particular object as the thing that he sees or is thinking about. Such a suggestion may always be rejected, though sometimes this will appear perverse. But the acceptance of such a suggestion must not be misunderstood. Suppose *A* says 'I was thinking of a window with three pointed internal arches supported on round columns: in particular I was thinking "A window with three ..., etc., supported on round columns must look pretty silly"'. Now if *B* gets *A* to agree that he must have been thinking about the window at York – though this has square columns – *B* (or indeed *A*) may say '*A*(I) was thinking about the window at York, the one with three pointed arches supported on square columns'. This is a (*b*)-statement and mention of any property of the window at York may replace the descriptive phrase in it. Once we have a statement about what *A* was thinking about which identifies a particular object, inferences of the form '*A* was thinking about *X*, *X* is a *P*, so *A* was thinking about a *P*' may be multiplied. All the statements will be (*b*)-statements.

But these (*b*)-statements and (*b*)-inferences about what *A* was thinking about have no bearing upon *A*'s original statement of what he was thinking about – his statement of his thoughts. The truth of the (*b*)-statement '*A* was thinking about the square-columned window at York' in no way conflicts with the (*a*)-statement '*A* was thinking about a window with round columns'. Having a thought, *P*, part of which is expressed by such a phrase as 'a round-columned window', and which

17

is therefore about such a window, in some circumstances *constitutes, or is held to constitute*, thinking about a particular window and all the things that window is, e.g. square-columned. To draw the conclusion that there was no thought about a round-columned window would be absurd, for it was this that constituted thinking about a square-columned window.

There seems an exact parallel here with seeing. Seeing certain colours and shapes (e.g. a green square) *may* constitute, or be held to constitute, seeing a grey wall, though it need not. In this case there will be two answers to the question what was seen, one an (*a*)-statement and the other a (*b*)-statement. Since seeing the green square was what constituted seeing the grey wall, it would be absurd to argue that no green square was seen. To claim that since no green square existed none could have been seen is to confuse the denial of a (*b*)-statement with that of an (*a*)-statement.

Notice also a further difference between the two statements 'I see a green square' and 'I see a grey wall', *as they occur in the example above*. The first implies 'I see green', whereas the second does not imply 'I see grey'.

The opinion that there exists such a distinction between 'see'-statements may be reinforced by the following argument:

(1) (According to Warnock) If A sees X and X is red, A sees a red X. It does not however follow that A sees red – the colour. There is no valid inference from 'A sees X and X is P' to 'A sees the property, P, of X'. The same argument applies for all perceptible properties of X.

(2) But if A sees at all, A must see a colour, shape, light and dark.

(3) It follows that:

    (i) It must be possible for A to see a colour that is not the colour of any particular object he sees – and is not even the apparent colour of any particular object he sees (for 'A sees X and X appears Q, so A sees something which has a Q appearance or appears Q' is valid); and the same goes for shapes.

    (ii) There must be true statements, about someone, A, who sees something, of the form 'A sees a CX' (where CX is, e.g., a coloured shape), which cannot

18

be interpreted as inferences from, or as equivalent to, statements of the form, '*A* sees an *X* which is *C* though *A* is unaware of *C* or of its being *C*'.

One cannot make this point, however, in terms of a distinction between the sentence forms '*A* sees a *CX*' and '*A* sees an *X* which is *C*'. The sentences,

'*A* wants a poisonous drink',
'*A* wants a drink which is poisonous',
'*A* sees a red chair',
'*A* sees a chair which is red',

may all express (*a*)-statements, i.e. may not express statements about particular objects. Similarly,

'*A* wants what is, in fact, a poisonous drink',
'*A* wants a drink which, as a matter of fact, is poisonous',
'*A* sees what is, in fact, a red chair',
'*A* sees a chair which, as a matter of fact, is red',

may all express (*b*)-statements, i.e. may all express statements about particular objects. But we need to put in the phrase 'as a matter of fact' to begin to make the difference.

One more point on the general question of Warnock's thesis (1). Austin[2] argues that, although I may see a blurred shining patch, or two lines when there is only one, really I should say 'I see a shiny object blurredly', or 'I see a line double'. The point seems to be that I should deny that I see two things, while yet conveying that I see two-ly.

If we compare seeing a black line double, triple, quadruple, etc., with seeing it single, there is plainly a difference in what is seen. At the extreme it may be the difference between seeing a little black and seeing nothing but black. If there may be such differences in what we see it would seem proper to report the fact explicitly. In such a case we see, on the one hand, one line to which we and others can point ('*That* one') and, on the other, several lines to which we cannot point, so that if we are asked 'Which lines?' we cannot answer (though we can, and in psychological experiments often do, refer to them individually, as 'The one on the left', etc.).

On the whole I agree with Warnock that the inference pattern,

'A sees X, X is P, so A sees P',
seems to be correct. But so do the inference patterns,
'A wants X and X is P, so A wants P' and
'A thinks about X and X is P, so A thinks about P',
so long as one is careful not to slip from 'an X' to 'a particular X' and back.

The treatment of the man shaved in Oxford, however, raises some problems. In
'A sees X and X is Y-ing, so A sees X Y-ing'
the conclusion is ambiguous; one is inclined to say ambiguous between
'A sees something, X, which is Y-ing' and
'A sees *something Y-ing*'.
But the point is not to be made, as Warnock sees, by distinguishing seeing an X Y-ing from seeing an X which is Y-ing. If that were the point it would be puzzling why there is no real difference between 'seeing a red X' and 'seeing an X which is red'. The distinction is between seeing a thing or object and seeing an event: 'A sees a thing, X, X is being Y'd, so A sees a Y-ing' is an invalid inference from seeing an object to seeing an event. The identity statement should be 'X is something being Y'd', and the conclusion 'A sees something being Y'd'.

This sort of point makes it clear why, when I see a bag of marbles, it cannot be inferred that I see marbles. A 'bag of marbles situation' is a 'marbles in a bag situation' but a 'bag ...' is not a 'marbles...' Ayer's[3] arguments from incomplete perception seem also to involve errors of inference of this type: 'I see an apple, an apple is flesh and pips, etc., so I see flesh and pips, etc. But I don't, so I don't see the apple'. But, of course, though an apple is composed of flesh and pips, it is not flesh and pips (nor is it a back and a front, an inside and an outside).

But there seems still to be a difficulty. Consider the following inferences:
'A sees that tree and that tree is standing in a park, so A sees a tree standing in a park',
'A saw John, John was covered with spots, so A saw John covered with spots'.
'Standing in a park' and 'being covered with spots' are not

events, yet the inferences both seem to me unsound. The conclusions imply that both the tree and the park, both John and his spots, were seen, yet the premises do not entail this. If it is argued that a tree is a thing but a tree standing in a park is a situation, then why, when a chair is a thing, is a red chair not a situation? One is tempted to introduce a 'which'-clause to make the distinction.

Why should it be true that
  'If I see an X and X is a P, I see a P'?
Compare
  'If I touch X and X is a Y, I touch a Y'.
This can be explained, not by the fact that I need know nothing about something in order to be said to touch it, but by the analysis of touch, viz. 'A touches B'='A part (or surface) of A is in spatial contact with a part (or surface) of B'. Now, if X is a part of Y and Y of Z, X is a part of Z, and if X is a part of Y and $Y = Z$, X is a part of Z. Comparable explanations of the transitivity of seeing might be:

(1) 'I see X'='X is before me ($+$I am sighted)'; of course if X is before me and X is a Y, a Y is before me;

(2) 'I see X'='X induces a belief in me, etc.'. Again, if X induces a belief and X is a Y, then a Y induces a belief.

In fact I do not believe analyses of these two kinds to be satisfactory. However, Warnock's account of the speck that is a star suggests another line:

(3) 'I see an X' (where 'an X' refers to a particular thing existing in time and space)='I see colours and shapes which are the appearance of a particular thing, X, or which are what some particular thing, X, appears to me as'.

Now, if X is a Y, then whatever X appears as, a Y will appear as. Moreover, if we accept Warnock's account of the speck, if I see what X appears as I see X. This account makes use of a primitive 'see'-sentence of the form 'I see a colour or coloured shape'. I do not believe this can be analysed further. It is, however, a sufficient condition of the *capacity* to see colours and shapes that a person satisfactorily discriminates colours and shapes and acquires the appropriate linguistic ability. Statements of particular perceptions, e.g. 'I see a red square' or 'I see red now', like 'I have a pain', may be uttered by and accepted from those who have shown a capacity to distinguish colours or pains and use colour or pain words correctly. But they are unanalysable. The question whether what I see is what some particular thing X appears as is surely a pragmatic one.

In conclusion I shall list a number of distinctions which appear to be involved in this subject but which may rather easily be confused:

(1) What A sees/what A thinks he sees.
(2) What A sees/what (particular thing) A sees.
(3) What A sees (the intentional object)/what A sees (the material object).
(4) What A sees/what A *actually* sees.
(5) Seeing a thing/event/property/situation.
(6) Seeing a part/aspect/whole/a thing.
(7) Seeing a QX/seeing an X which is Q.

Notes

1. G. E. M. ANSCOMBE, 'The intentionality of sensation', in R. J. Butler (ed.), *Analytical Philosophy*, second series (Oxford, 1965).

2. J. L. AUSTIN, *Sense and Sensibilia* (Oxford, 1962), p. 92.

3. A. J. AYER, 'Has Austin refuted the sense-datum theory?', in *Synthese*, vol. 17 (1967), p. 125.

An Analysis of Perceiving in Terms of the Causation of Beliefs

I

J. W. ROXBEE COX

I INTRODUCTION

In this paper I try to work out in some detail an analysis of perceiving of the 'causal' variety. It is a causal account of perception in the sense that the account sketched by H. P. Grice in his 'The causal theory of perception' is a causal account.[1] According to such an account, he writes, 'the elucidation of the notion of perceiving a material object will include some reference to the role of the material object perceived in the causal ancestry of the perception (or of the sense-impression or sense-datum involved in the perception)' (p. 121). My account differs from Grice's in two important respects. First, it is not restricted to the case where we are said to perceive a material object (or to perceive any other kind of object). In fact it takes as the fundamental concept for perception perceiving-*that* something is the case. Secondly, it does not make use of any such notion as that of a sense-impression or sense-datum. It is an account in terms of the causation of *beliefs* – that is, of their acquisition or retention. It is thus more akin to the views proposed by D. M. Armstrong.[2] However, his statements of a causal account must appear, even to a sympathetic reader, to contain two very fundamental deficiencies. First, his characterization of perception as 'the acquiring of true or false beliefs about the current state of our body and environment by means of the senses' is open to the objection that his characterization of the notion of the senses itself makes use of the notion of perception.[3] My account of perceiving-that avoids this circu-

23

larity. The second deficiency is that, as he himself admits, he cannot formulate necessary and sufficient conditions for someone's perceiving a *thing* in terms of the notion, asserted to be basic, of perceiving-*that*.[4] To do this is, of course, one of the main tasks for an account of perception that seeks to challenge the more usual assumption that perceiving things is the fundamental case, in terms of which perceiving-that can be elucidated.

The main views I shall elaborate may be briefly (and therefore somewhat inaccurately) stated in the two following theses. (1) For a man to perceive that-p is for the state of affairs where-p to bring it about that he believes that p, where the circumstances that bring this about satisfy certain complex conditions. The main requirement here is that he learns what he does by exercising a capacity for identifying certain kinds of circumstance in which reliable beliefs are aroused. This thesis is elaborated in Section II. (2) For a man to perceive a thing, a y, is for him to perceive that some thing, a z, which is in fact the y, is at a certain place, while he is at the same time in a position to perceive 'directly' that the z has various properties and stands in certain relations to other things. Perceiving things, and perceiving things happening, will be discussed in Section III, with special reference to the sense of sight. The distinction between 'direct' and 'indirect' perceiving will be introduced in the course of Section II.

(The account of perceiving proposed here will apply to each of the senses. There are, however, points of detail that would have to be discussed separately for the separate senses. Considerations of length have therefore led me to restrict my discussion mainly to the case of seeing.)

It will be convenient to say something in advance about a familiar objection to which any account such as this lays itself open. In particular I must explain why I do not attempt to deal with it at all fully, while recognizing that it presents a fundamental problem for my analysis. The objection is that an analysis of perceiving in terms of the causation of beliefs will not be applicable to perceiving by infants and animals. We describe infants and animals as seeing things, when they are at stages of development at which we should not be prepared to ascribe to them beliefs (thus we say that a baby has seen the light moving, although we will not be prepared to say that he has acquired any beliefs, or that he thinks something or other to be happening). And in the case of animals to which we may be prepared to ascribe beliefs, we shall not be prepared to ascribe to them the complex and sophisticated beliefs that will be required by an analysis of perception. (Thus, it will be found that the account I propose requires someone who perceives *that* something is the case to have some view about the justifiability of his belief that it is the case; and such a belief cannot be attributed to an animal.)

Although a general reply to this objection may be possible, equally applicable to a number of different accounts of perceiving in terms of the causation of beliefs (and I shall myself suggest one such reply), the question of how far any specific account of this kind is able to deal convincingly with the objection may be expected to depend upon the details of that account. Furthermore, if the working out of the analysis shows it to have other attractions, such as an ability to deal with difficulties that seem intractable for some alternative views of perceiving, this will in itself increase its plausibility and make it seem worthwhile to go on to consider more fully the question of how far it can deal with the objection. I shall suggest at the end of Section III how far the analysis proposed in this paper is vulnerable to the objection; while in the next paragraph I mention one general line of defence that may have some plausibility. But I do not pretend to have rebutted the objection.

If we discover conditions that are necessary and sufficient for a man's perceiving a thing, but which do not appear to be necessary conditions for an infant's or an animal's perceiving a thing, we might suppose that the attribution of perceiving to the infant or animal was based on the creature's exhibiting in its actions and responses *many* of the features that are found in human beings who perceive things, but not *all* that variety of features. That is, we might suppose that the notion of perception was attenuated in its application in such cases. Although such a suggestion would require substantial arguments in its support before it was worthy of acceptance, the fact that there are undoubtedly cases where the notion of perceiving is attenuated in its application to adult human beings (as my examples near the end of Section III illustrate) may lend the suggestion some plausibility.

Before entering on the main argument of the paper, I may mention here two preliminary points, in order to prevent misunderstandings. First, the word 'perceive' is used in this paper in a technical sense common in philosophical writing, as a device that enables one to state briefly something that applies equally to each of the senses. Thus, for example, instead of saying 'When x sees that p, then ...; and when x hears that p, then ...', and so on for each of the senses, I shall say 'When x perceives that p, then ...'. I do not intend to express any views about the nature of perceiving, where this is understood in its less technical (and perhaps less common) sense. Secondly, a more substantial warning may be given about the exact nature of the priority I shall be claiming for perceiving-that. I shall be arguing that the *concept* of perceiving-that is fundamental, in that the concept of perceiving a thing can be explained in terms of it, whereas the converse is not true. I shall not be suggesting that the world is or could be such that people perceived that various things were true, but never perceived things. It will be found that when someone perceives that something is the case, he will also perceive some thing, or something happening.

II PERCEIVING-THAT

I wish to elicit the conditions that are necessary and sufficient for a man's perceiving that p. I shall start by considering a case that satisfies some of the conditions that are clearly necessary for perceiving that p, but which also clearly lacks some of the conditions that are necessary. I shall go on to consider further related cases where more conditions are satisfied until a case is reached that appears to be an example of fully-fledged perception, where conditions that are sufficient for perceiving that p are satisfied. This will be a case of what may be called 'direct perceiving-that'. It will be possible to analyse with the help of this notion a second kind of case of perceiving, which may be called 'indirect perceiving-that'. Since any case of perceiving-that which is not *direct* perceiving-that will be *indirect*, we will thus have a disjunctive set of conditions that are both necessary and sufficient for perceiving-that *p*.

It will probably be agreed that the following three conditions must be satisfied if it is to be true of someone, *x*, that he perceived that *p*. (Examples of what may replace '*p*' would be: 'there is a man at the door'; 'the painter has gone'; 'it is going to rain'.)

   (i) *p*;

  (ii) *x* came to believe (or to retain the belief) that *p*;

 (iii) the existence of the state-of-affairs-where-*p* brought it about that *x* came to believe (or to retain the belief) that *p*.

Two minor comments may be made about these conditions. First, one may take condition (iii) as adequate by itself, since it presupposes the truth of the first two conditions. However, it will be useful, for clarity and for purposes of comparison with other sets of conditions, to have the elements distinguished in this way. Secondly, it may be suggested that it is possible to analyse knowledge in terms of beliefs that are true, well grounded, etc., and that therefore condition (ii) could be stated in terms of knowledge. This may well be correct; but it will be convenient to employ the more non-committal formulation in terms of belief and the causation of the acquiring of belief, rather than a formulation in terms of knowledge and the causation of the acquiring of knowledge, until nearer the end of the Section.

Conditions (i)-(iii) are not sufficient to make it true that *x* perceived that *p*. If I measure a cube and then calculate its volume, then my belief that it has that volume might be said to be brought about by the existence of the state of affairs consisting in its having that volume; but I would not be said to have perceived that it had that volume. Among the many examples that could be given of cases where these three conditions are true but where *x* will not have perceived that *p*, I wish to look at an easily imaginable, even if unrealistic, case (Case 1) in order to see what features would have to be added to it in order to make it a case of perceiving that *p*.

Case 1

Suppose that a man, Jones, has lacked since birth the physiological equipment necessary for smelling things. He cannot ascribe odours to things near to or around him except, for example, by learning through what he *sees* or *hears* that a thing has a certain smell. Suppose now that surgeons operate on him and bring about a state of affairs where the presence of gas in the room in which he is causes him to acquire the belief that there is at that time gas in the room. Conditions (i), (ii) and (iii) are satisfied, and it may at first glance appear that Jones can now perceive that there is gas in the room. If the surgeons have achieved their success through restoring the functioning of the physiological equipment that normally enables a man to perceive odours, we may be very strongly inclined to say that he can perceive that there is gas, indeed that he can smell that there is. Even if the surgeons' success is due not to making the usual organs work, but to causing the gas to affect the brain without any part of the surface of the body being especially involved in the process, we may still be inclined to say that he can perceive that there is gas, although in an unusual way. In fact, however, the physiological detail is not important here, since the description of Jones's situation that has been given so far does not justify us in describing him as perceiving that there is gas in the room where he is. Although we have supposed there to be a *causal process* of a kind familiar in perceiving, Jones's *beliefs* are in an important respect not those of someone who perceives something to be the case. It is surely a necessary condition for perceiving that *p*, that the perceiver should believe that his belief that *p* has been brought about by the state of affairs where *p*. In the present case we have not attributed to Jones any view about how his belief has been brought about. For all that has been said, he might, for example, think that he *remembered*, on the strength of information that he had been given earlier, that the room would at that time have gas in it. I suggest therefore a fourth condition:

(iv) *x* believed that (iii).

(This is to be read as '*x* believed that the existence of the state-of-affairs-where-p brought it about that ...'. Here and elsewhere I insert hyphens where it will avoid ambiguities.)

Case 2

Case 2 will be specified by the conjunction of conditions (*a*) and (*b*). Let us suppose, first, that (*a*) the gas produces the belief that there is gas, in the same way as in Case 1; and that Jones believes that his belief has been brought about through the presence of gas affecting some part of the surface of his body (the part that is in fact affected). Condition (iv) is therefore satisfied. Will this be a case of perceiving that there is gas present? In the course of discussing this, we shall notice alternative cases that might be covered by (*a*), and shall go on to complete the specification of Case 2.

In order to answer the question, we may first ask whether or not Jones will have any reason to trust the belief that is aroused in this way. Supposing that he does have reason to trust it, we may then ask what grounds he has for relying on the belief; and the question of whether or not the case is a case of perceiving will depend upon the sorts of grounds he has for relying on the belief. We may complete the specification of Case 2 by supposing that his grounds are the following, rather unusual, ones.

(*b*) Jones has been told that a sudden conviction occurring in him at 9.45 a.m. will have been brought about through the experimenters having used their technique to affect a part of the surface of his body in a certain way, and that what affects his body will in fact be the existence of a state of affairs that he will then come to believe exists. If he trusts his informant, he may then not only have the *sudden* conviction as predicted, but also come to believe for more than a moment that there is gas in the room, and that the presence of the gas has aroused in him this belief through the gas's affecting the surface of his body in a certain way.

Case 2, specified by (*a*) and (*b*) together, differs from the normal case of perceiving in an important way. We have supposed that Jones's reason for believing for more than a moment that there is gas present is that he believes that the sudden conviction that occurs is to be relied upon; and his basis for this belief is that he trusts the person who told him this was so. We may contrast this kind of reason for relying on the belief that is aroused with the reasons one will have in an ordinary case of perceiving that something is the case. In the ordinary case, the grounds for relying on the belief that is aroused have something to do with the actual character of the belief itself, or of the circumstances in which the belief is aroused. In the present case, the reason has to do with external features of the circumstances in which the belief is aroused. This point will be clarified and developed in connection with the next case.

Case 3

Case 3 will be specified by the conjunction of the conditions (*c*), (*d*) and (*e*). Suppose (*c*) that the description (*a*) of Case 2 still applies: the belief is aroused through Jones's body being affected, and he believes that this is how the belief is aroused. Conditions (i)-(iv) are satisfied. Suppose further that, instead of its happening on an isolated occasion, (*d*) Jones frequently has beliefs aroused in this way, and knows that this is so, and is able to identify the occasions on which beliefs are aroused in this way, when they occur. Will this make any crucial difference? There are two possibilities to consider here. One is that he knows that the same process is involved on each occasion, because he is told on each occasion. That is, there is frequent repetition of cases like Case 2, just considered. We need not consider this further, as repetition will clearly not confer on such cases the character of perceiving. The other possibility that we must consider, and which will complete the specification of Case 3, is that (*e*) he is able to recognize that the various occasions on which he comes to have these beliefs have something in common, and that this feature generally indicates that the belief acquired is reliable.

If he recognizes that these occasions have something in common, this feature might be one of two kinds. It might either be a feature of the circumstances in which the belief was acquired, or it might be a feature of the content of the belief itself. Thus, to illustrate the first possibility, it might be suggested that the *experience* one has when perceiving with a certain sense that something is the case is characteristic of perception with that sense, and that this will provide a common feature that would enable a person to identify a particular occasion as of a kind where the beliefs that are acquired are in general reliable. The second kind of feature is illustrated by what may be called the 'characteristically perceptible properties' corresponding to a particular sense. In the case of sight, for example, if we perceive something to be the case, we will come to believe that something has a certain colour or light property, where our justification for believing this is *not* that it can be inferred from something else that we believe.[5] We may interpret condition (*c*), therefore, as requiring either that Jones had an experience characteristic of those occasions when the gas affected his body and produced the belief that there was gas, or that there was some property such that on all these occasions he acquired the belief that the gas had this property, where his justification for believing this would *not* be that it could be inferred from something else that he believed.

Once Jones has come to be able to recognize these situations as sharing a feature, in either of the ways just suggested, then, if he has reason to think that beliefs aroused in circumstances having this feature are in general reliable, he will on a particular occasion of this kind have a reason for thinking the belief reliable. It is clear that if the feature he goes by is of either of the kinds just suggested, then his grounds for relying on the belief aroused will be very different from his grounds for relying on the belief in Case 2, where he was going on the word of an informant. In the present case, he relies on his experience, and perhaps the experience of others too.

At this point we must take up certain questions about the acquisition of beliefs, the postponement of which may have made the discussion so far appear somewhat unrealistic. It may seem that the discussion has represented the perceiver as a passive recipient of the end product of a causal process. Indeed, a causal account of perception might appear committed to just that view. On the other hand, the concept of perceiving is surely the concept of the exercising of a capacity; and not just a capacity for being at the receiving end of such a process.

I must therefore emphasize and elaborate the element that has already been introduced that corresponds to the capacity element in perceiving.

Let us suppose that Jones had in fact *not* found any reason to repose confidence in the beliefs that are acquired in the rather peculiar situation that we have imagined to exist in Case 3. We might then feel that the situation would be less misleadingly described as one in which the gas affects the surface of the body, and thereby gives rise, not to beliefs, but to momentary beliefs, convictions, feelings, or inclinations to believe, that something is the case. Because of their unreliability, they are, at least after a little experience of such situations, rejected, so that Jones does not in fact acquire a belief, if this is taken to mean something more than a momentary belief. The cases where he does actually acquire a more than momentary belief will be ones where he thinks he has good grounds for accepting the belief. (In general, if a man believes that *p,* then he will believe that he has good grounds for his belief.)

The causal account of the acquisition of beliefs in perception will be oversimplified if it leaves out this consideration. I do not wish to suggest, on the other hand, that perceiving will involve three stages – the acquiring of a short-lived belief, the checking of its credentials, and its acceptance as a longer-lived belief. This will only be true of rather unusual circumstances, as where a man stumbles upon a scene so extraordinary that he can hardly believe his eyes. Normally, we know in advance that our situation is one in which we will acquire beliefs in certain familiar and trusted ways, and we are prepared in advance to accept the beliefs that are acquired, so long as the circumstances of their acquisition are not unusual.

Thus our general knowledge and preconceptions will usually lead us to accept without question the beliefs that we acquire. It is, similarly, such general knowledge and preconceptions that may lead us on certain occasions to reject, or at least to question, certain momentary beliefs that are acquired. We may therefore reject certain sudden feelings, bursts of confidence, inclinations to believe, hunches, etc., on such general grounds as that there is no solid reason for believing such a thing; that, in situations of the kind one is in, people are often inclined to believe things that there is no good reason to believe (as with sickness, drugs, etc.); or perhaps that what one is inclined to believe is so improbable that it can safely be rejected, as when a lecturer disregards the evidence of his own eyes that there is a tiger seated in the audience, on the general grounds that it is more likely that he is wrong, even though he cannot at present see how, than that there should be a tiger sitting there.

Turning back to the main line of argument, I suggest that where, as in Case 3, Jones correctly identifies the circumstances in which the belief is aroused as having a certain character, and where he also correctly believes that beliefs aroused in such circumstances are reliable, then he will be justified in holding the belief that has been aroused. If we suppose further that conditions (i)-(iv) are satisfied, and that Jones's own reason for relying on the belief aroused is his confidence in the reliability of beliefs aroused in such circumstances, we have the core of a set of conditions that, I suggest, are sufficient for perceiving, although not necessary; they are the core of a set of conditions both sufficient and necessary for a kind of perceiving that we may call 'direct perceiving-that' ('DP'), in terms of which it will be possible to analyse another kind of case, which may be called 'indirect perceiving-that'. I set out first the seven conditions that have already emerged, to which we shall see two further conditions will have to be added:

x directly perceived that p if and only if:

DP (i) p;

(ii) x came to believe (or to retain the belief) that p;

(iii) the existence of the state-of-affairs-where-(i) brought it about that (ii);

(iv) x believed that (iii);

(v) the way in which the state-of-affairs-where-(i) brought it about that-(ii), had a character that x identified correctly as s;

(vi) x believed correctly that beliefs aroused in this way are in general reliable;

(vii) since x believed that beliefs aroused in this way

33

are in general reliable, he did not reject the belief that (i).

In our example of Jones in Case 3, the following replacements may be made in the conditions:

'p': 'there was gas in the room where Jones was';

'x': 'Jones';

's' might be something like 'involving the peculiar experience he had when acquiring beliefs on previous occasions O_1, O_2, O_3 and others'; or something like 'involving his coming to believe that something had a certain oxygen content and a certain colour, where his justification for holding these beliefs was not just that the presence of these properties could be inferred from other features that he knew the thing to have'. (At this point we may give up the supposition, made in (a) of Case 2 (and retained in Case 3), that Jones believes that the way in which the state of affairs where there is gas present brings about his belief that there is gas present is through the gas affecting some part of the surface of his body. The belief in the role of the body does not appear necessary, so long as condition (v) is satisfied in some way or other.)

Of the two further conditions that must be added, the first is connected with the point mentioned at the beginning of the Section, that condition (ii) should perhaps be formulated in terms of knowledge, rather than belief. Thus the following objection can be made against the conditions so far listed; they might all be satisfied, without it being true that x perceived that p – if his belief that p is based on a false belief, and is thus a lucky accident. For example, a man might think that he had seen that a gun had fired, when what had happened was that a gun had fired making a flash that he did not see to occur, and that the firing of the gun had surprised a photographer into letting off a flash bulb, the flashing of which the man mistook for the flash of a gun.[6] It seems that perceiving-that is not merely a matter of acquiring true beliefs in certain ways, but also a matter of acquiring true beliefs on good grounds that do not include false beliefs – in fact a matter of acquiring knowledge. We might therefore be inclined to replace (ii) by '*x* came to know that *p*'. However, later conditions are concerned with the causation of the belief mentioned in (ii); and what is mentioned in the later conditions may not provide an explanation of the acquisition of knowledge, since what accounts for knowledge must be concerned with matters of justification as well as matters of causation. It will be better, therefore, to add a separate condition. A possible candidate would be: '*x*'s belief was not based on any false beliefs'. However, while this would deal with the particular loop-hole brought out by the example, it fails to deal with the general difficulty of which the example is a manifestation. To the extent that accounts of knowledge in terms of justified true belief are inadequate, seeming to require continuous accumulations of conditions, so may we expect this account of perceiving-that to reveal corresponding inadequacies. It may therefore be more realistic to add the following condition with its implied reference to the possibility of defining knowledge in terms of justified true belief:

(viii) the circumstances in which *x*'s belief-that-*p* was acquired were not such as to disqualify it from being called knowledge, through (for example) including in its grounds beliefs that are false, or true but irrelevant, etc.

The last of the conditions to be added is more directly important for the problems of this paper. It is sometimes true that when a man perceives that *p*, there will be something else that he perceives to be the case (that q), from the perception of whose truth he is entitled to conclude that *p*. Such cases may naturally be called 'indirect perceiving-that'. In our description of Jones's situation in Case 3, he has *not* perceived indirectly that there is gas in the room. He has not been described as having perceived something else to be the case from which he is entitled to conclude that there is gas. Such a case may be called 'direct perceiving-that'. (In what follows I shall in fact call such cases 'direct' and 'indirect perceiving', since we shall not have occasion to make a distinction between direct and indirect perceiving of things and happenings.) The final condition for direct perceiving may be stated thus:

(ix) it is not the case that x could have had, as his only reason for not rejecting the belief that p, the fact that there was a state of affairs (viz., that where q), which he has come to believe exists, and from whose existence he correctly believes that he is entitled to conclude that p.[7]

It should be noticed that condition (ix) does not entail merely that when someone actually goes through a process that may be described as inference, then he does not perceive directly. The class of cases where he does not perceive directly will include cases where there is no reason to think the perceiver has gone through an inference, but where it is still true that his reason for not rejecting the belief that-p would be that there were things he could perceive to be true, from which he *would* be entitled to conclude that p. Thus many cases of perceiving, which it would be highly implausible to represent as involving inference, will count as indirect. For example, if I see that there is a typewriter on a table in front of me, it may well be the case that there are things I see to be true and from whose truth it should be possible to infer that there is a typewriter on a table before me: that there is a brown thing of a certain shape and size before me, etc. If this is correct, then I shall have seen indirectly that there is a typewriter on a table in front of me.

At this point we may naturally ask what states of affairs are members of the class of states of affairs that we may directly perceive to exist. From what has been said so far, it appears that there may be no *general* answer to this question. What one man may perceive directly to be the case, another may perceive indirectly (with the same sense) to be the case. We shall expect very complex states of affairs to be identified for what they are through indirect perceiving, and certain very simple ones, such as that something is reddish in colour, through direct perceiving (on most occasions).[8] Apart from such rough generalizations, the question must be answered for individual instances – by, for example, questioning the person involved. Fortunately, for the purpose of the present discussion, all we need be able to assert generally is that certain kinds of feature will be directly perceived in normal cases by any normal person: thus that a thing has a certain colour of a very familiar kind, or a shape roughly of some familiar kind, that one thing is moving relative to some other thing, etc., are among the things that one will be able to see directly to be the case when one sees something. That a sound has a certain broadly described timbre and loudness is something that one who hears it will directly hear to be the case. Again, one will be able to see directly that a thing is in a certain direction from where one is, and that it is at a great or small distance from one. (This is not paralleled for the case of hearing; sometimes, but by no means always, one can tell that a sound is coming from a certain direction, and is near or far away, as the case may be.)

In order to see what conditions will be satisfied by the kind of perceiving that may be called 'indirect perceiving-that', we may take two examples of cases that are obviously not cases of direct perceiving:

(α) Jones saw that it would be fine on the following day, from the fact that the sky was pink, etc.

(β) Jones saw that the Smiths were away, from the fact that their windows were all closed, the gate shut, etc.

In case (α), conditions DP (i) and (ii) will be satisfied; condition (iii) will not be, since the state of affairs where it is fine on the following day will not bring about the earlier belief. On the other hand, we shall expect Jones to perceive directly something to be the case, namely that-q, from which he would be entitled to conclude that it was going to be fine: that is, we shall expect the negation of DP (ix) to be true, and further that his reason for accepting the belief will actually be of the kind excluded in DP (ix). However, as our example of seeing the table to be present shows, the negation of (ix) can be true when it is *also* true that conditions DP (i)-(viii) are true. In such a case there will be something that he directly perceives, that q, which could provide a basis for the kind of inference mentioned in DP (ix). Example (β) also enables us to bring out the fact that the question of whether his belief was brought about, even indirectly, by the state of affairs where-p (that is, whether condition DP (iii) holds), is not the crucial one. It could have happened that the departure of the Smiths had brought about the closing of their windows, etc., by someone else. But whether or not this was so is clearly not relevant to the issue of whether Jones saw directly or indirectly that they were away. He will have seen this to be so in the same way, whatever explanation of the closing of the windows, etc., is correct.

From the consideration of these examples, we can go on to formulate a list of conditions that we shall find almost complete for what may be called 'simple indirect perceiving' ('SIP'). (As the last two conditions listed here will be replaced, I shall asterisk them.)

SIP   (i) p and q;

       (ii) x came to believe (or to retain the belief) that p;

      (iii) x perceived directly that q;

     (iv) the-state-of-affairs-where-(iii) brought it about that (ii);

    (*v) since x believed that from the-fact-that-q he is entitled to conclude that p, he accepted the belief that p;

   (*vi) the belief mentioned in (*v) is correct.

It will be convenient to indicate at this point why the conditions mentioned would only be conditions for a certain *simple* kind of case of indirect perceiving. In each of the examples (α) and (β) it may well be argued that the plausible candidates for the role of the state-of-affairs-where-q will themselves not be directly perceived to be the case. In such cases there will be at least one intermediate state of affairs, that where-s, which is perceived to be the case and which is related to the state-of-affairs-where-q in the way that the state-of-affairs-where-q is related to the state-of-affairs-where-p in simple indirect perceiving – with the qualification that 'directly' must be replaced by 'simply indirectly' in condition SIP (iii).

Conditions SIP (i)-(*vi) are not by themselves enough to make a case of acquiring a belief a case of indirect perceiving. In some cases that satisfy these conditions a man will be said to have *concluded* that p, or to have *realized* that p, but not to have *perceived* that p. For example:

(β') Jones realized that the Smiths were in Switzerland; from the fact that the windows were all closed, etc., and from

38

the fact that if they went away before 1 April they were to go to Switzerland, while if they went away after that they were to go to Austria.

We may compare this example with a slightly simpler one, intermediate between (β) and (β'):

(β'') Jones could see that the Smiths were in Switzerland from the fact that the windows were all closed, etc., and the fact that whenever they go away they go to Switzerland.

In case (β'), although the inference may be justified on this occasion, it is not one that can be backed by a generalization in the way that the inferences corresponding to (β) and (β'') are. It is not just the complexity of the inference corresponding to (β') that stops it from being a case of seeing-that, but the fact that the inference does not belong to a class of inferences that could be made in similar cases. While I cannot put the point as precisely as would be desirable, I suggest that we must add to the conditions already mentioned a further one, that whenever x perceives that a state of affairs like that where-q exists, he is entitled to infer that a state of affairs exists like that where-p. We can in fact incorporate this in condition (*v), so that the conditions for x perceiving in the simple indirect way that p will be:

SIP (i) p and q;

(ii) x came to believe (or to retain the belief) that p;

(iii) x perceived directly that q;

(iv) the state-of-affairs-where-(iii) brought it about that (ii);

(v) since x believed that whenever he perceives that there exists a state of affairs that is in certain respects, k, like that where q, then he is entitled to conclude that there exists a state of affairs in certain respects, k', like that where p, x accepted the belief that p;

(vi) the belief mentioned in (v) is correct.

Given this set of conditions for *simple* indirect perceiving, it is easy, though cumbersome, to formulate the conditions for a hierarchy of cases of indirect perceiving that may be called complex.[9]

III PERCEIVING THINGS HAPPENING AND PERCEIVING THINGS

The views proposed in the present section are more controversial than those just developed. Briefly – and, we shall see, too simply – my thesis is that one perceives a y when one perceives that some thing, a z, which is in fact the y, is at a certain place, and one is in a position to perceive directly something about what it is like, what it is doing, where it is, what its surroundings are like, etc. (Perceiving *what* it is like is, of course, a matter of perceiving *that* it has this, that and the other property, etc.)

My procedure will be, as before, to approach the somewhat complex set of conditions for perceiving things, by first taking a rather simple view that is clearly not correct, and then modifying and adding to it in order to arrive at a satisfactory set of conditions. For simplicity I shall deal first with those comparatively straightforward cases of perceiving things happening where the perceiver does not make any mistake and is not in any doubt. Later I shall suggest how the conditions must be qualified to take account of some of the less straightforward cases where errors or doubts of one kind or another enter in.

The main kinds of case to be covered are these: first, perceiving something happen or perceiving something happening; second, perceiving one thing in a certain relation to another thing (a dog behind a gate, for example); and third, perceiving a thing. For the first group, I shall talk of perceiving a y a-ing: seeing a dog pass, hearing a dog barking, for example. The relational case will not require more than a brief mention. The case of perceiving a thing I shall talk of as perceiving a y. In the first part of the discussion that follows immediately I shall be dealing with all these cases together, and will abbreviate mention of all of them by using such expressions as 'perceiving a y a-ing' or 'perceiving something (happening)'.

The simplest suggestion that might be made about the connection between perceiving-that and perceiving things (happening) is that where one perceives a y a-ing, one perceives *that* there is a y a-ing, and vice versa. But this is easily seen to be wrong. If Jones saw the computer building, he need not have seen that it was a computer building, or even that it was a building; if he saw soldiers drilling, he need not have seen that there were soldiers drilling; if he heard a train passing, he need not have been able to tell that there was a train passing. And, as has been seen in the preceding section, Jones can see that there is a train passing, without seeing a train.

These examples may prompt a second suggestion. This is the view that although he need not perceive that there is a y a-ing, he will perceive that there is a z b-ing, where the z b-ing is the y a-ing. Thus he may see only that there is some large thing before him, where the large thing is the computer building. He may have seen that there were people moving about, where the people moving about were the soldiers drilling. He may have been able to hear only that some heavy machinery was operating in the vicinity, where the heavy machinery in operation is the train passing.

This suggestion has the merit of being able to deal with such cases as that where, in the situations just mentioned, Jones wrongly thought that he could see a Gothic chapel in front of him, or that there were children playing at soldiers before him, or wrongly thought that he had heard a dam burst. Although these beliefs are not correct, his having them will involve him in having certain beliefs that are correct: that there was a building before him, that there were people moving about, and that something in motion had made a loud noise. It can also deal with such cases as that where Jones saw that there were twinkling specks down in the valley, where the twinkling specks were the soldiers. In this kind of case, in order to show that the z b-ing is the y a-ing, we must show that the state of affairs where there was a y a-ing brought about the acquisition of the belief that there was a z b-ing, and also that the place where x would locate the z b-ing is the same as the place where the y is a-ing. (The question of the location of the state of affairs where the z is b-ing we shall return to later.)[10]

So far the following conditions have emerged for someone perceiving something (happening) ('PH'). x perceived a y a-ing if

(1) A y was a-ing at a place v at a time t;
(*2) x perceived that a z was b-ing;

41

(3) the z b-ing was the y a-ing.

(It may be useful to state explicitly that one can perceive a y a-ing without its being true that a state of affairs where there is a y a-ing is one that can be recognized as such by sight. This has in fact already been illustrated with the example of the computer building.)

We may elicit the further conditions for 'x perceived a y a-ing' by contrasting two kinds of perceiving and asking what the difference is between them. One case is that where a man perceived *that* a certain thing was going on, but did not actually *perceive it going on*. The other is where he perceived *that* it was going on, and *also perceived it going on*. We may take two pairs of examples, one involving something happening, and one involving relations between things.

Suppose that Jones entered a room and saw that there was a fire burning in the grate, from the flickering light reflected on the walls and furniture, but did not actually see the fire burning in the grate because his back was to it. If we now suppose him to have turned round so that he was facing the fire, not only will he have seen *that* there was a fire burning, but he will also have actually seen the fire burning. We may ask what will have been present in the second situation and absent in the first that might correspond to the difference that we are interested in.

A second pair of examples. Suppose that Jones saw that the painter was in the dining room, from the fact that sheets lay across the floor at the door, etc., but did not see the painter in the room. Suppose, secondly, that Jones moved to a position where not only was he able to see *that* the painter was in the dining room, but he could also actually see the painter in the dining room. What are the important differences between the two cases?

We might naturally point to the following difference in the fire example (which is paralleled in the painter example). When Jones was facing the fire, he was in a position to see what the state of affairs (the fire burning in the grate) was like in various respects: he could see whether there were tall flames, whether they moved quickly or burnt steadily, what colours the various parts of the fire were, what was next to the

42

fire and what was above it, and what the spatial relation was to himself of the place where the fire was burning. In the case where he was facing the wall opposite the fire, on the other hand, it appears that he would not be in a position to see that this variety of things was true.

However, the contrast is not quite as clear-cut as this. It must be admitted that when facing the wall Jones might in fact be in a position to see, for example, that there were fast-moving flames, that it was a small fire, and that the place where the fire was burning stood in a certain spatial relation to himself; even though there appears to be a limit, reached quite quickly, to the things that he could perceive to be true of the state of affairs in question. (Corresponding qualifications of the contrast may be found for the painter example, also; but they will be less obvious.)

Having admitted this much, however, we must notice also that there can be cases where the man who is not described as seeing a thing happening is in just as good a position as the man who is so described to perceive what the thing (happening) is like, etc. Suppose, for example, that a man sees a uniformly blue sky, which fills his field of vision when he looks straight upward: he will be in a position to see that the sky is uniformly blue and very bright. Suppose now that he looks through a periscope from an enclosed room, and can tell from the image in the periscope that straight above is a uniformly blue and bright sky; or again that he looks not through a periscope but at an instrument whose reading gives him the same information. It is not true that there are things that he is in a position to perceive to be true of the thing in question when he sees it which he is not in a position to perceive to be true of the thing in these cases where he does not perceive it.

The contrast that we are here trying to formulate can be stated with the help of the distinction between direct and indirect perceiving. Two possible ways of putting it suggest themselves. We might, first, modify condition (*2), making it 'x perceived directly that a z was b-ing'. This might be objected to on the grounds that it could be true that the things that a man actually perceived to be the case with respect to a thing that was before him were none of them ones that he could *directly* perceive to be the case. However, it is surely difficult to deny that when *x* perceives a *y a*-ing, there will be *some* values for 'a *z b*-ing' such that the *z b*-ing is the *y a*-ing, and he directly perceives that there is a *z b*-ing. For example, he might directly perceive that there was something going on in front of him, where what was going on was cows going across the road.

Some might feel disinclined to rely on this reply. The second suggestion that makes use of the distinction between direct and indirect perceiving will avoid their objections, and is also of interest and importance in its own right. This is the suggeston that we retain (*2) as it stands, and add a further condition:

(4) *x* was in a position to perceive directly that the state of affairs where the *z* was *b*-ing had certain features, and that the place where the *z* was *b*-ing stood in a certain spatial relation to himself.

The correctness of this condition is brought about if we reformulate what was said in the first attempt to make the contrast between the case of the man facing the fire and the case of the man facing the wall opposite the fire, prefixing the occurrences of 'see' by 'directly'. Clearly, when his back is to the fire, he will not be in a position to see *directly* that things are true of the fire and its burning. What he will be in a position to see directly, on the other hand, will be what the flickering on the wall is like.

If we add this condition we can leave (*2) as it stands. But could we leave (*2) out altogether? It will be useful to consider briefly the view that it should indeed be dropped. It might be argued that while perceiving a thing (happening) does require condition (4), that is, requires the *possibility* of acquiring beliefs if certain conditions are satisfied, perceiving a thing (happening) does not require that the perceiver *actually* acquires a belief. One argument in favour of this view was mentioned and commented on in Section I: creatures can perceive at a stage of mental development at which they cannot have beliefs. I discuss this issue again very briefly at the end of the present Section. A second argument is that if we are very abstracted, for example, we may not acquire any belief when we perceive something. We may stare out of the window and not see that anything in particular is the case. In reply to this, we may mention again such very general beliefs as that there is something of some colour in the direction we are facing, or that it is day and not night. Must we not acquire (or be confirmed in) some such beliefs? The argument is in any case less plausible in the case of hearing than in the case of seeing. If a man heard something happening, he must have acquired certain beliefs about the occurrence of sounds. If he was only *in a position* to acquire such beliefs, but did not in fact acquire any, we should say rather just that he was in a position to hear what was going on. (The kind of case I have in mind is that where, for example, I am so engrossed in my reading that I do not hear the conversation or the repair work that is going on outside the door of my room, even though it is within earshot.) I suggest therefore that condition (*2) is necessary. We need not decide whether the emended version, where the perceiving is said to be direct, is also correct. The discussion suggests that if we add condition (4) to the three already listed, the case of perceiving a *y a*-ing will be adequately distinguished.

A word must be said in explanation of the expression 'in a position to' as it is used here. This is intended to embrace certain possibilities: if certain conditions were to be satisfied, he would perceive directly that such-and-such was true. The possibilities in question are perhaps most easily indicated by considering how we would explain his not having seen that the state of affairs had a certain feature, when he saw the state of affairs in question. There seem to be two main kinds of explanation: either he lacked the *knowledge* to recognize what was before him as answering to a certain description, or else his *attention* was always elsewhere. The knowledge condition is straightforward enough. The 'attention' condition is more difficult to state in an informative way. Taking the case of sight, we may put it by saying that if, for example, he had not been looking at something over to the other side of the region where the *z* was *b*-ing, or if he had not been thinking very hard about something else, or if he had not been concentrating on what he could *hear* going on, he would have seen directly that such-

and-such was the case. What we are saying in condition (4), therefore, is that if x's attention were not elsewhere or absent, and if he was able to recognize that kind of feature, then he would have perceived directly that the state of affairs had certain features. What is *not* covered by 'his being in a position' to perceive directly that such things are the case is, for example, its being true that if a cloth were lifted off a bird cage, he would directly perceive that there was a yellow object over to his left.

The specific conditions for perceiving something in a certain relationship to something else may be got by making minor replacements in the statement of the general conditions for perceiving a y a-ing. The same is true for the case of perceiving a y, where the perceiver is not described as perceiving it a-ing or in a certain relation to something else. When we come to consider this case, however, it becomes clear that condition (*2) is incomplete, although it happens that this is not so obvious for the other cases we have dealt with under the general formula, 'perceiving a y a-ing'. A simple substitution in (*2) for the case of perceiving a thing will give 'x perceived that there was a z'. When we recall that 'a z' will be replaceable by such expressions as 'a pile of sheets', or 'a fire', the inadequacy of the formulation is clear: x will obviously perceive something more specific to be the case, namely, that a particular z exists at a particular time and place. Clearly condition (*2) must be completed by bringing in a reference to the time and place at which the z exists (and, in general, at which the z is b-ing). There are two ways in which this might be done. One would be to expand the condition to 'x perceived that a z was b-ing at v at t'; that is, the spatial and temporal identifications used in (1) would reappear in (2). The objection to this is that in condition (1) the time and place may be specified in one of any number of possible ways, including, for example, the giving of precise scientific identifications. It is obviously not necessary that x should be able to identify the place and time of the z b-ing in any such way. Although he may identify the place, for example, in a way that does not implicitly mention his own location ('south of Helvellyn', for example), it will clearly be quite satisfactory if his identification

46

does make implicit reference to himself, as in 'before me', 'within earshot', 'over to my right', etc. A general term to cover these cases would be 'in my vicinity'. A corresponding temporal reference would be 'now'. For convenience we may take both of them to be covered by the expression 'in my vicinity'. Thus (*2) will become:

(2) *x* perceived that a *z* was *b*-ing in his vicinity.

In making explicit in this way the need for some such expression as 'in his vicinity' in condition (2), it may appear that we are admitting a circularity into the account of perceiving something (happening). For must not 'in his vicinity', 'before him', etc. (as these expressions are to be understood here), be elucidated as meaning something like 'at a place perceptible from where he is'? If so, the notion of perceiving a thing may appear to have entered surreptitiously into its own analysis.

This is not in fact so. It is possible to give an analysis of 'before him' or 'in sight' (to take examples for the sense of sight) in terms of seeing-that, or, more specifically, seeing-directly-that. If *x* saw that there was a dog before him, this could of course have been indirect perceiving. But the use of 'before him', etc., here is such as to require that the place where the dog is seen to be was one at which things could be *directly* seen to occur. The analysis of this, in accordance with the conditions set out in Section II, does not make use of the notion of perceiving. Thus there is no circularity.

(It emerges from this point, incidentally, that condition (4) is in fact already implicit in condition (2). Since condition (1) is already implied by the conjunction of (2) and (3), we could take these two conditions as giving the analysis of '*x* perceived a *y* *a*-ing'. It is more helpful, however, to distinguish these different elements in the analysis.)

Our ability to locate the things that we might describe as before us is a matter of experience. If we see that a dog is before us, that is, is at a place where we can directly see some things to be true of what is there, then it will have to be within something like half a mile; if it is a hill that is before us, it will have to be between a few yards and twenty to forty miles away (depending on its size and the conditions of visibility such as light or fog); if it is the sun or a star, it will be very much further away. The specific distance also on any particular occasion will be learnt by experience. That a thing is a hundred yards away, or five minutes' walk away, or ten miles away, is a relational feature of the thing that we learn to recognize in the same way as we learn to recognize other non-relational and relational features by sight.

For terrestrial phenomena, the time at which we can directly perceive things to be true of a thing will be more or less contemporaneous with the acquiring of the belief. For celestial phenomena the times will be different. The notion of 'temporal vicinity' must be extended to take account of this. If we are mistaken about the time involved we shall be partly mistaken in the perceptual belief. (Our analysis does not suggest that such a mistake will entail the falsity of the statement that we perceive the thing in question.)

The conditions that have emerged for perceiving something (happening) are these. x perceived a y a-ing, if and only if:

PH   (1) a y was a-ing at a place v at a time t;

      (2) x perceived that a z was b-ing in his vicinity;

      (3) the z b-ing was the y a-ing;

      (4) x was in a position to perceive directly that the state of affairs where the z was b-ing had certain features, and that the place at which the z was b-ing stood in a certain spatial relation to himself.

(The reference to 'perceiving' in the conditions must be understood to be a reference to seeing throughout, or to hearing throughout, etc.: not to seeing in condition (2) and to hearing in condition (4), for example.)

These conditions will fit satisfactorily those cases where we perceive something (happening) and where we are not mistaken in one way or another, and also those cases where we are mistaken because a thing looks to us other than it is. There are, however, certain cases where we are said to perceive things (happening) where these conditions will not be fulfilled. I shall mention four kinds of cases.

(A) *Waking and wondering.* It quite often happens that a man wakes in the morning, and wonders whether he actually heard a door close, or whether he merely dreamt it. If in fact

it was a door closing that woke him, and certain other conditions are satisfied (roughly, that a waking man where he was
would have heard it), then he will be said to have heard it. A
slightly more complex case is this. A packet of letters drops
through the letter box on to the wooden floor, and wakes him,
and in waking he wonders whether he heard a gun go off or
whether he merely dreamt it, or whether perhaps he heard
something else. He will be said to have heard the letters drop
to the floor. In neither of these cases will it be true that he
could hear that something-or-other: his state is one of wondering, not perceiving-that. Cases of this kind can also be found
for sight, though they may be less common: 'Did I see a flash,
or did I dream it?'

(A′) We may contrast this with a slightly different case.
Suppose that the postal packet lands noisily on the floor,
causing him to wake up wondering whether he had heard a cat
purring, or whether he dreamt it, or whether he heard something else. He will not be described as having heard the postal
packet land on the floor. It appears that the dissimilarity
between the sounds is too great in this case.

(B) *Dreaming.* Slightly different from these cases are those
of kind B, where a man awakes believing that he has just
dreamt that a gun has gone off (for example), when a postal
packet has landed on the floor. Again, if certain obvious
conditions were satisfied, he will be described as having heard
the packet land. But his state is one of remembering a dream,
not one of believing that something has happened downstairs.

(C) *'Did I imagine it?'* Often a man will wonder whether
he saw something move, over to one side of his field of vision,
or whether he imagined it. If something did move, he will be
said to have seen it.

(D) *Perky's case.*[11] In this psychological experiment, the
subjects were convinced that they were describing visual
imagery with their eyes open, when in fact they were describing
shapes that were projected before them on a screen. Their
error was due to a number of factors, including their expectation that they would have imagery and see nothing but a
blank screen. Here again, they must be described as seeing the
shapes, but it is not true that this involved them in perceiving-

49

that something was the case.

I wish to suggest that these cases satisfy certain conditions, which explain their being classified alongside the central cases of perceiving things, by noticing their similarity to the case where a thing looks to a man other than it is, with the result that he acquires a false belief about it, together with a number of correct beliefs. (I shall call this for brevity the 'appearance-case'.) We have already noticed that this will satisfy the conditions, PH, for perceiving a thing. We may compare it with a related case where a man would *not* be said to see the thing about which he acquired the false belief, and where he would be described rather as suffering from a hallucination.

Suppose that Jones looks across the room to where there is only a shaggy black dog, and thinks that he has seen a stainless steel towel rail. We shall be disinclined to say that he has seen the dog, and that it looked to him like a towel rail. There appears to be some limit on how a thing can look to a person, and where a man's belief about what he can see passes this limit, we are inclined to describe his situation in terms other than that of mistake. In the appearance case, a certain kind of explanation will be believed possible, which will account for the incorrect element in the belief. The incorrect belief that the thing before him has a feature, g, will be due to the thing actually having a feature, g', and to the operation of some distorting factor, which results in the presence of a g' thing leading the perceiver to believe there is a g thing present. In the case of the man who thought he saw a towel rail, we shall not expect an explanation that rests upon optical phenomena, or physiological or psychological factors, that cooperate with the presence of the dog in producing the belief. We shall rather expect an explanation, perhaps both physiological and psychological, that will account for the normal causal efficacy of the presence of the dog being completely counteracted.

A corollary of the claim that, in the towel rail case, the belief is not to be explained by reference to distorting factors is that the belief was not due to the exercise of the capacity for perceiving-that. In the ordinary appearance-cases, on the other hand, where distorting factors are present, the belief *is* the result of the exercise of the capacity for perceiving-that, an exercise that was partially unsuccessful because of the presence of these factors.

Turning to the cases A-C, it will be seen immediately that they share with the appearance-cases the two features just mentioned: in each case the state aroused differs from the belief that a normal perceiver at the same place would have had aroused, in a way that can be explained by reference to distorting factors that account for the exercise of the capacity for perceiving-that being unsuccessful. We may notice that in the case A', where the man wonders if he heard a cat purring when the packet lands on the floor, the explanation of the disinclination to describe him as having heard the packet land will be the same as in the towel rail case: this pair of conditions appears not to have been satisfied.

In case D, that of Perky's subjects, the distorting factor that combines with the exercise of the capacity for seeing-that to produce an erroneous belief, is of a kind different from the sources of error in the previous cases. In this case it is a matter of the people's preconceptions. Preconceptions can be a familiar source of error in appearance-cases also. Looking for a paper clip on the floor, I may take to be a paper clip something that in ordinary circumstances I would not mistake for one. My preconception about what I will find makes me take the other thing for a paper clip. (The preconception about a matter of fact will in this case no doubt be itself due to my *desire* to find the clip; a point that is not paralleled in the Perky case.) Thus the two features mentioned are present in this case also.

Before assessing the significance of the features shared by the appearance cases and the cases A-D, we must notice two important and related respects in which the A-D cases differ from the ordinary cases of non-mistaken perception, and also from the appearance-cases. First, the perceiving does not involve actually perceiving that something is the case. Secondly, in these cases the perceiver will not be in a position to perceive directly what the thing or happening is like. Thus it appears that although cases A-D are treated as cases of perceiving, they differ from the more normal cases very fundamentally.

In order to see why nevertheless the A-D cases are treated as cases of perceiving, we may notice a way in which they come *close* to satisfying these two conditions. Clearly, if the distorting factors had *not* been present, and things had been otherwise the same, then the subjects in our examples would have perceived something to be happening, and would also have been in a position to perceive directly what the thing or happening was like in a variety of ways. This is a relevant consideration, in a way in which 'if he had been ten miles away and in normal circumstances, he would have perceived that *q*' is not relevant. It is relevant because these are indeed *distorting* factors: other conditions for seeing were present, and in the absence of these special factors, the situation would have been the normal one.

The fact that cases which differ from the normal in this way are treated as cases of perceiving suggests that the concept of perceiving is one where great emphasis is laid on the operation of the causal process that gives rise to direct perceiving-that in the normal case. Once this process has taken place, then even if for some reason the resulting state is not direct perceiving-that, but is a false belief (as in D), remembering a dream (as in B) or wondering of one kind or another (as in the others), the case is still regarded as one of perceiving the thing or happening that brings about the belief or other state. We thus have a picture of a normal and central case of perceiving something (happening), where conditions (1), (2), (3) and (4) are satisfied, and of other cases, also counted as perceiving, where conditions (2)-(4) are not satisfied but where a much weaker set of conditions is satisfied, which share the fundamental elements just noticed with the central case. I would suggest then that the cases A-D are counted as perceiving because of their relation to the central cases of perceiving; as opposed to holding that all the cases share certain essential features equally, and that the A-D cases are just less common or less important. It seems possible to imagine a world in which we had our present concept of perceiving and in which such cases as the A-D cases never arose, but it does not seem possible to imagine a world in which we had our present concept of perceiving, and where the A-D cases existed but the normal cases did not.

The conditions that are satisfied by the cases A-D are these:

(1) a *y* was *a*-ing at *v* at *t*;

(2′) x came to be in a certain mental state (believing, wondering, etc.) through the exercise of the capacity for perceiving-that;

(3′) certain factors were present such that, (a) together with the existence of the state-of-affairs-where-(1), they brought it about that (2′), and such that (b) if they had not been present, the state-of-affairs-where-(1) would have brought it about that (2), (3), and (4).

This is a convenient place at which to try to estimate how far the present account of perceiving is open to objections to analyses of perceiving in terms of the acquisition of belief of the kind that was mentioned in Section I. The difficulty centres most obviously on condition PH(2). According to the present analysis, to say that a dog saw a cat is to imply that the dog saw that something was the case, where this in turn implies that the dog had certain sophisticated beliefs of the kind mentioned in the conditions for direct perceiving (DP(i)-(ix)). Assuming that we are not prepared to modify the conditions, the present analysis of perception can only be defended along the lines suggested in Section I. It is also relevant, however, to consider what sorts of modification of the conditions might also enable us to deal with the difficulty; for the conditions are complex enough for it to be possible that an analysis having broadly the same character, but with differences in the detailed conditions, should be more defensible than the one that has been presented here.

One possibility would be to omit condition PH(2) altogether. We have seen that this might be proposed for quite different reasons. If this were to turn out to be correct, then we should have to commit ourselves only to the view that the dog was *in a position to* see that certain things were the case. Exactly how this could properly be interpreted is too large an issue to go into here. It might perhaps be understood as allowing for the possibility that, if the dog were (what it is not) the possessor of certain sophisticated concepts, that is, were more like a human being than it is, then if certain other conditions (the same as for men) were satisfied, it would acquire certain beliefs.

Another, more radical, modification would be to accept PH(2), but to modify the conditions for direct perceiving, in particular conditions DP(iv)-(ix), so as to omit or qualify references to the perceiver's views about the justification of his belief. Although I have not been able to propose such a simplified set of conditions, I am not unsympathetic to the suggestion that such a modification might be correct. This is because my conditions for direct perceiving may seem unnecessarily strong, implying as they do a greater mastery of the notion of the reliability of a belief than some may think necessary.

IV APPLICATION TO SOME DIFFICULT CASES

The character of the present account of perceiving, and how it differs from other recent causal accounts, may be illustrated by a brief consideration of some cases that have provided difficulty for those accounts. I shall first mention a general difficulty, which is satisfactorily dealt with on the present account; and then I shall discuss some examples that have been found to present difficulties for these accounts, hoping to show that they can be accommodated by the account proposed here.

The general problem is formulated by Grice as follows: [12] 'In any particular perceptual situation there will be objects other than that which would ordinarily be regarded as being perceived, of which some state or mode of functioning is causally relevant to the occurrence of a particular sense-impression: this might be true of such objects as the percipient's eyes or the sun.' He then mentions Price's suggestion that we should distinguish between 'standing conditions' and 'differential conditions' here.[13] Standing conditions would include the state of the sun, for example. If a standing condition was suitably altered, 'all the visual impressions of the percipient would be different from what they would otherwise have been; whereas the state of the perceived object is a differential condition in that a change in it would affect only some of the percipient's visual impressions, perhaps only the particular impression the causal origin of which is in question'. The suggestion then is that the causal theory should hold that 'an object is perceived if and only if some condition involving it is a differential condition of some sense-impression of the percipient'.

Grice points out that this will not deal with the difficulty. For example, a change in the state of a concealed torch (its being extinguished, for example) may be restricted in its effects to the particular thing illuminated by that torch, while things lit by other torches remain unaffected. The state of the concealed torch would count as a differential condition; yet we should not want to say that we saw the concealed torch. Grice's own tentative suggestion is that the causal theorist should merely indicate by examples the character of the causal connection that exists between a perceived object and a percipient, leaving it to scientific investigation to discover what in fact the connection may be.

Grice discusses this problem in connection with a causal theory in which the notion of a sense-impression has a central part: it is sense-impressions whose occurrence is caused by the things that we are said to perceive. But it is clear that a corresponding problem may exist for a causal account that, like Armstrong's and like the present one, is formulated in terms of the causation of beliefs. Armstrong's account does not provide an answer to the problem. I wish to show that the present account does. We may divide the discussion of the problem into two parts. (I) When a *state of affairs*, described as the state of affairs where *p*, is causally responsible for *x*'s perceiving that *p*, in what circumstances will it also be true that *x* *perceived that p*? (II) When an *object*, *y*, is such that its presence or absence, or its state, is causally relevant to *x*'s perceiving that *p*, or perceiving a thing, *z*, or perceiving something happening, in what circumstances will it also be true that *x* will have perceived that thing, *y*?

The answer to the question (I) is implicit in the discussion in Section II above. It may be most readily brought out with an example. If my eyes are in reasonably good health, then I shall be able to see what is going on around me in conditions that are otherwise suitable for seeing things. Suppose I wake in the middle of the night: I might ask myself, 'Is it pitch dark? Or am I blind?'. I can learn that my eyes are in good health by switching on a light and finding out whether I can then see things around me. If I can, I shall also have learnt that my eyes are in working order. Furthermore, the way in which I will have learnt this is such as to satisfy the conditions for indirect perceiving-that.

We may contrast with the fact that my eyes are in working order certain other states of affairs that will also hold if I am to see anything, but which I will *not* perceive to hold when I see something. Whereas it is common knowledge that one's eyes must be in order if one is to see, there are many conditions that must be satisfied with respect to the visual system that are not known to, for example, me. Although these are causally requisite for my seeing something, it will not be true that I learn that any specific one of these conditions is satisfied when I see something. An eye specialist can, of course, see that a great number of them are satisfied when he sees things. Only those causally relevant factors whose presence I can learn of in the ways satisfying the conditions for perceiving-that will be ones that will be perceived to hold; and these will have to be ones that are identifiable by me when they exist.

We may now turn to question (II). When will it be true that an *object*, some state of which is causally relevant to our perceiving something, is itself perceived? We have just seen that most of us will see such things as that the sun is illuminating the room, or that it is cloudy, or that the electric light is on, on most occasions when we see anything. But can we state the conditions, in terms of our account of perceiving, that such 'causally relevant' objects as the sun, clouds or the lamp are to satisfy if we are to be said to see *them*? (I shall restrict the present discussion to cases of seeing.) We may illustrate how these questions are answered on the present account by taking some cases discussed by R. Firth.[14] (He is considering the suggestion that a sufficient condition of seeing something is that light from that thing transmits light to the perceiver, which affects his 'visual experience'. He points out that we can find cases where such transmission of light will be involved in perceiving, but we can also find cases where the transmission of light occurs in the same way but where we do not perceive the source of the light.)

56

Firth describes certain pairs of contrasting cases. One set of cases concerns translucent media. Thus (A1) if we are looking into the water round a boat, and the presence of the sand and kelp on the sea bed produces 'changes in the color of the sea under our boat', we are not said to see the sand and kelp. Again, when we turn our face towards the sun on a bright day with closed eyes, 'our field of vision is sometimes suffused with a pinkish glow'; in such circumstances we are not said to see the sun. On the other hand (A2) we are said to see objects through glass that is not transparent but is translucent. Firth does not give an example of this. I imagine the kind of case he has in mind is where we see people in a restaurant through misted windows.

Cases of reflected light also provide contrasting examples. (B1) When we are reading a book, and light from the book has its source in the sun or a lamp, we are not said to see the sun or the lamp. If some of the light reaching our eyes from the book has been reflected from a wall on its route from the sun, we are not said to see the wall. (B2) On the other hand, when we look in pools of water or in looking glasses, where the light has been reflected as in the other cases, we are said to see our faces.

The 'light transmission' view cannot account for these differences. If the present account is to be more successful, it must presumably show that the things mentioned (the sand and kelp, the thing behind the translucent glass, the sun, etc.) will in cases A1 and B1 fail to satisfy the conditions for being seen given in Section III, while in the other cases, A2 and B2, the things mentioned will satisfy the conditions.

The question to ask then is whether, given that there is at a certain place a y, it is true that there is a z such that we perceive that the z is in our vicinity and are in a position to perceive directly what the z is like in certain respects, and such that the z is the y. In some cases it will be found that the last condition is not satisfied, which will show that we do not have an instance of seeing the y.

(A1) In the sand and kelp example, we see that there is a certain pattern of colours in the water under the boat; is it true that the pattern of colours is the sand and kelp? Surely not.

We may compare with this the case where we see through transparent water that there are patches of various colours on the sea bed, and where we are in a position to see directly that they have certain properties and relationships to other things. Here it may be true that the patches of colour are the sand and the kelp; and thus that we see the sand and kelp, even though we cannot identify them as such.

The case where we look with closed eyes towards the sun, and see that there is a pinkish expanse before us is like the sand and kelp case. The pinkish expanse is not the sun. Thus we cannot be said to see the sun. We may compare with this the case where we look towards the sun at sunset, and see that there is an oval red patch in the clouds; and where it is true that we are in a position to see directly what the red patch is like, and in what relation to us it stands. The oval red patch may be the sun; in which case we shall be said to see the sun. (We determine whether it is the sun in accordance with the conditions suggested in Section III.)

(A2) In the example of people in the restaurant with misted windows, what we see is that there are shadows of certain shapes and degrees of definition on the glass, and we are in a position to see what these shapes are like in certain respects and what spatial relationship to ourselves they stand in. Are these shadows on the glass the people inside the restaurant? Perhaps the answer is 'Yes'. If so, then perhaps we can be said to see the people. However, one may doubt whether the sense in which the shadows could be said to be the people is the one we are concerned with. In saying that the shadows are the people we may be making the same sort of claim as when we point to part of a photograph and say that that is the Queen. If that is all we are saying, then it will not follow that we see the people in the restaurant. What Firth requires, if he is to provide contrasting cases where light is transmitted through translucent media, are examples. If my suggested example does not do the job, then this merely means either that other examples can be found, or, if not, that the problem cannot be illustrated with this class of cases.

(B1) In the cases of reflected light not involving a mirror, what we see to be the case, about which we are in a position to see that certain things are true, is that there is a certain distribution of light of a certain character before us. The question is whether this distribution of light is the sun (or a lamp, or the wall); and the answer is 'No'.

(B2) For the case of seeing a thing in a mirror, it will be convenient to take as the example, not seeing my own face in a mirror, which is Firth's example, but a less special case, such as that where I see a chair in a mirror. We must ask then what I see to be at a certain place when I look in a mirror, of which it can be said that it is a chair, and about which I am in a position to see directly that it has certain features and that it stands in a certain spatial relation to myself. If we suppose that the chair itself satisfies these requirements, we imply that in such a case I can see directly what it is like, and where it is with respect to where I am. Against this it may be pointed out that it will always be possible to explain how I can learn that the chair has such a feature or stands in such a relationship by reference to the reflection of the chair that I perceive to be before me in the mirror. Thus it appears that I shall not be in a position to see directly that anything is true of the chair in this case. What satisfies the conditions, then, will be the reflection that I see to be before me, and perhaps also a shape that I see to be before me within the frame of a mirror. Of either of these it can be said that I see it to be before me, and that I am in a position to see directly what it is like in certain respects; but can it be said that the reflection or the shape is the chair, in the sense that will satisfy condition PH(3)? The answer appears to be 'No': for the requirement that the z should be located by x at the place where the y is will not be satisfied. (Indeed, the sense in which the reflection or the shape can be said to be the chair seems to be the sense in which the shape in the photograph can be said to be the Queen.)

Someone who disagrees with this last point, about the sense in which it can be said that the reflection is the chair, may draw the conclusion that the account of seeing a thing given in Section III enables us to explain the contrast noted by Firth, and say that, where the light reaches our eyes from a thing after being reflected from a mirror, we shall see that

59

thing. However, my position is that we cannot show that the case of seeing something in a mirror counts as a case of seeing that thing, according to the account of seeing given in Section III. There are now two ways in which the argument might be continued. It might be claimed that since in fact we do not, strictly speaking, *see* things that we are said to see in mirrors, the use of the criterion given in this paper merely gives results consistent with the facts. Even if this first claim were accepted, however, it would still leave another question demanding an answer: why is it that, even if seeing in a mirror is not strictly speaking seeing, it can for many purposes be treated as if it was a case of seeing of the straightforward kind.

It will be of interest to consider whether the present account suggests an answer to this second question. There are two main features that distinguish seeing a chair in a mirror from other cases of seeing that a thing is at a certain place when we do not actually see that thing. First, the man who sees a chair in a mirror will be in a position to learn about the chair and its surroundings very much the same variety of things that could be learnt by someone looking straight at the chair from a suitably selected viewpoint. This may be called the 'same knowledge' feature. Secondly, a *description* of what he can see to be before him by the man who is looking in a mirror will also be largely applicable to what would be seen to be before him by a man who looked at the things reflected in the mirror, from a suitably selected viewpoint. Effects of the light on the mirror's surface, imperfections in a looking glass, ripples on the surface of a pool, etc., will cause their descriptions to differ in certain respects. We may call this the 'same description' feature. We may discuss the significance of these two features more fully.

Same knowledge. Of special importance is the fact that, when I look in a mirror, I shall be able to say what the spatial relation to me is of the thing whose reflection I see, without having to make use of any information other than that gained through sight on that occasion. I see that there is a mirror, and thus, seeing that there is before me and to the right the reflection of a chair, I see that the chair itself is to my right and some way before or behind me (as the case may be). Again – a point it would not normally occur to one to emphasize – I shall know that the time at which the chair occupies that position is the time at which I am looking in the mirror. We may contrast with this the case where I learn of the place and time of some occurrence through seeing a television picture of it. Supposing that I can see that it is a television picture, as in the other case I can see that it is a mirror, it will not be true that I thereby learn at what time and place the occurrence took place or is taking place. The same point can clearly be made about films, photographs and paintings.

If we suppose that the acquisition of knowledge about what is happening or has happened at a certain time and at a certain place is an important feature of perceiving, then the fact that this feature is shared by seeing a thing in a mirror and seeing that thing without a mirror, will justify contrasting these two cases with the other cases. Since the account of perceiving elaborated in this paper does suggest that the acquisition of knowledge about what is perceived is a fundamental element of perception, our account will provide some reason for assimilating seeing a thing in a mirror to seeing that thing.

Same description. The importance of the 'same description' requirement may be brought out if we try to imagine a device that will satisfy the 'same knowledge' condition without satisfying the 'same description' condition. Although such devices do not exist, they are easily imagined, and the following description would appear to specify one: a device like radar, in which the picture is not representational, but which enables us, by looking at the device, to learn about a thing exactly the same detailed information as could be learnt about it by looking at it directly from some reasonably good point of view. The information would include the temporal and spatial relation of the thing to the person looking at the device, this information being acquired through looking at the device, in the knowledge that it is a device of that kind. I think it will be agreed that we would not be said to see the things we learnt about in this way 'in' or 'through' the device. If we now suppose the device to be improved by the 'picture' being made representational so that the 'same description' condition is satisfied, we are supposing it to become similar to instruments with which we are very familiar, such as periscopes and telescopes; and it is clear that we should be happy to talk of seeing things 'in' or 'through' the device, just as we talk of seeing things in a mirror, or through a telescope. The 'same description' requirement thus seems as necessary as the 'same knowledge' requirement.

The account of perceiving proposed in this paper does not, however, suggest why the 'same description' requirement should hold. Thus, while this account can *help* to explain why seeing things in mirrors should be treated as virtually seeing those things, it does not succeed in suggesting why other imaginable devices should not also be treated like mirrors in this respect, when, as we have seen, they would not in fact be so treated.

In view of this failure, it cannot be claimed without qualification that the analysis proposed is able to deal with all the kinds of cases that have presented difficulties for other causal accounts. On the other hand, the case of seeing things in mirrors is a very special case. Inadequacy in only this respect should not, I think, weigh too heavily in the balance against the ability of the account to accommodate other cases that have presented difficulties for causal analyses.

Notes

1. H. P. GRICE, 'The causal theory of perception', *Proceedings of the Aristotelian Society*, supp. vol. 35 (1961).

2. D. M. ARMSTRONG, *Perception and the Physical World* (London, 1961), ch. 9, and *A Materialist Theory of the Mind* (London, 1968), ch. 10.

3. *A Materialist Theory of the Mind*, pp. 210-12.

4. *A Materialist Theory of the Mind*, p. 230.

5. In my paper, 'Distinguishing the senses' (*Mind*, 79 (1970)), I argue against the first of these alternatives, and elaborate an account that gives a central position to the 'characteristically perceptible properties' corresponding to a particular sense.

6. I owe this example to Dr Aaron Sloman.

7. We say here 'his *only* reason' and not just 'his reason' in order to

deal with the kind of case where a man may have more than one justification for coming to believe that *p*. Thus I might see that a certain light is red, and be able to give as a reason for believing it to be red the fact that it is the top light of a set of traffic lights. But if it is also true that if I had seen only the red light, or had not known that the top light of a set of traffic lights is always red, I should still have acquired the belief that it is red, and should *not* have been in a position to conclude that it was red from something else that I came to believe on that occasion, then the perception that it is red will count as direct. Here it will not be true that my only reason for thinking it red is that I believe I am entitled to conclude that it is red from something else that I believe.

8. Cf. G. E. M. ANSCOMBE, 'The intentionality of sensation', in R. J. Butler (ed.), *Analytical Philosophy*, second series (Oxford, 1965), pp. 174-5.

9. We noticed the case where the conditions (SIP) are altered by the replacement of 'directly perceived' in (iii) by 'simply indirectly perceived'. If we treat simple indirect perceiving as first order indirect perceiving, we may call this case of complex indirect perceiving 'second order indirect perceiving'; and we may formulate a third order case by similar substitutions. More generally, the conditions for indirect perceiving of the order *n* ('IP$_n$') will be:

    (i) p_1 and p_2 ... and p_{n+1}
    (ii) *x* came to believe (or to retain the belief that) p_1;
    (iii) *x* indirectly perceived (order *n*-1) that p_2;
where (iii) will involve that
        x indirectly perceived (order *n*-2) that p_3;
and so on down to
        x directly perceived that p_{n+1}.

10. The fact that I take 'The twinkling specks were the soldiers' as an instance of 'the *z b*-ing was the *y a*-ing' shows that the 'is'-relation in condition PH(3) that follows, is asymmetrical. Condition (3), which is fundamental for the present account, is clearly in need of more elucidation than is offered here. I imply that the fact that the soldiers' presence may contribute to bringing about a belief entitles us to say that the twinkling specks' presence contributed to bringing about a belief. While I think this is all right, I realize that what appear comparable cases of substitution of this kind would be highly suspect. In J. L. Austin's classic example, my saying 'That white dot on the horizon is my house' would not license the conclusion that I live in a white dot (*Sense and Sensibilia* (Oxford, 1962), p. 98). (It might perhaps license the conclusion that I live in *that* white dot.) For discussions of this problem see, e.g., P. F. Strawson, 'Perception and

identification', *Proceedings of the Aristotelian Society*, supp. vol. 35 (1961), J. M. Hinton, 'Perception and identification', *Philosophical Review*, 76 (1967), P. Alexander, 'Inferences about seeing', *Royal Institute of Philosophy Lectures, Vol. III (1968-69), Knowledge and Necessity* (London, 1970), and the contributions by Warnock and Taylor in the present volume.

11. C. W. PERKY, 'An experimental study of imagination', *American Journal of Psychology*, 21 (1910).

12. H. P. GRICE, 'The causal theory of perception', *Proceedings of the Aristotelian Society*, supp. vol. 35 (1961), pp. 142-4.

13. H. H. PRICE, *Perception* (London, 1932), p. 70.

14. R. FIRTH, 'The men themselves; or the role of causation in our concept of seeing', in H. N. Castañeda (ed.), *Intentionality, Minds and Perception* (Detroit, 1967), pp. 379-82. I do not undertake to discuss here the class of cases suggested by Grice's example of the torches, since they are unusually complex, as the following remarks will indicate.

It might be argued that in some such cases a perceiver can see directly that the torch has certain features, and occupies a certain position relative to himself: for example, it has a yellow beam, is very bright, is moving and is about ten yards to his right. On the other hand it might be said that even in cases where this information is available to the perceiver, that thing about which the perceiver is able to see directly that certain things are true is not in fact the torch, but the light cast by the torch. (Compare the case where we might say, 'We could see the cigarettes of the guests in the darkened garden', where all that could be seen were the glowing tips of the cigarettes.)

II

WILLIAM KNEALE

I

Roxbee Cox has raised many interesting questions, but I shall not attempt to discuss them all, because I want to concentrate attention on something he does not discuss in detail but notes in passing as an assumption implicit in his suggestions for analysis of the notion of perceiving, namely the proposition that animals and human babies cannot rightly be said to perceive anything in the full sense of the word 'perceive' that interests him. This seems to me very strange for various reasons.

In the first place, it is contrary to the general consensus of mankind, both learned and simple. At the beginning of the fifth century B.C. Alcmaeon of Croton, who certainly counts as one of the learned, since he was the first person to look for connections between the sense organs and the brain, said, as though he was stating something obvious, 'Man differs from other animals in that he alone understands, while the rest perceive but do not understand.' And in this he was followed by almost all philosophers before Descartes. As for the simple, Roxbee Cox himself admits that we all describe animals and infants as seeing things we see, and he mentions nothing in our common practice to indicate that we think of such talk as involving a departure from our ordinary standards for the use of the word 'see', though his theory requires that there be such a departure. It is true that when I say that my cat sees a book that I have left lying on his favourite chair, I do not want to suggest that he recognizes the thing as a book; for I know that no being who lacks a language can understand what a book is. But there is no difference of kind between this case and many cases in which human beings are said to see things of sorts of which they have no concepts. It is a commonplace that before the

65

development of modern geology many people in limestone districts saw the ossicles of fossil crinoids without realizing that these little cylinders, which they called St Cuthbert's beads, were remains of marine organisms. And in our time, as Roxbee Cox will agree, a man may see a computer without knowing its name or understanding its nature.

Next, a large part of my own perceptual life is of a sort I find no difficulty in attributing to animals. When, for example, I walk along the road thinking of the day's news or of what to say in a philosophical paper, I preserve my balance and choose my direction by reference to the things I see around me, adjust my step according to the feel of the ground under my feet, and jump to the side if I hear a honking noise behind me. Perhaps my behaviour may be described as a sequence of unreflective responses to stimuli. Certainly it is not the outcome of internal debate; for I do not even think to myself as I go along 'There is a wall. There is a sheep. There is a muddy patch on the road' or 'Now the right leg. Now the left.' But all the while I am aware of the changing situation, and my awareness does not consist in the holding of the hypothetical truth that I could, if questioned, say what I have just said. On the contrary, my special human ability to talk correctly about what is going on seems to me to depend on my seeing, feeling, and hearing fairly well in the same way as I suppose my cat to see, feel, and hear. If I became blind, numb, or deaf, I should not be able to walk along the road safely; and the same goes for him, though he might be rather better off, because his sense of smell is better than mine.

Finally, if, as seems obvious, the only difference between ourselves and animals or infants that might conceivably be cited in support of Roxbee Cox's doctrine is that we have language whereas they have not, it is impossible to understand in his scheme how we, who were once infants, succeed in learning a language. The germ of truth in Wittgenstein's denial of the possibility of a private language is that all natural language must start with talk about common perceptible objects such as men, animals, trees, and stones. But creatures who were unable to perceive such things would be unable to learn words for talking about them; so it seems preposterous, in the original sense of that word, to suggest that they might acquire an ability to perceive by first acquiring a language.

If, as it seems to me, Roxbee Cox has committed himself to theses that conflict with commonsensical views about the position of man in the animal world, the reason may be that he has confused two different things, namely the having of a perception and the making of a perceptual claim. Obviously anyone who says that he sees something must have an idea of seeing; but it does not follow that, even for a person who says that he sees something, the seeing that he ascribes to himself involves use of the idea of seeing, as promising involves use of the idea of promising. And *a fortiori*, when we say that the cat saw a mouse, we do not by that statement credit the cat with an idea of seeing, though we may sometimes be inclined to say other things about him that do *prima facie* imply that he has an idea of seeing, as, for example, that he moved in order to see the mouse better. Since, however, we all learnt to use the word 'see' in situations in which people recounted and discussed what they could see, it is not surprising that we sometimes find it difficult to separate the notion of seeing from that of thinking correctly that we see. When trying to analyse the notion of seeing, we very naturally ask ourselves 'What do we mean when we say that we see something?' and after raising this question we may easily slip into talk about the state of mind of a person who says that he sees something. I think that this is an unfortunate move, but that Roxbee Cox is not the first to make it. In order to get the contrast clear, let us consider two accounts of perception that are separated by nearly five hundred years.

In his *Summa Theologiae*, I, q. 78, a.3, St Thomas Aquinas tells us:

Sense is a receptive faculty, naturally subject to change by an external sensible. It is therefore the external source of change that is directly perceived by sense and through its variety allows for distinction of the different senses.... For the operation of sense there is required a change in the soul by which an appearance [*intentio*] of a sensible form is produced in the organ of sense.

And in the next article he adds:

But it is necessary for an animal to seek, or flee from, some things not only because they are agreeable, or disagreeable, but also on account of other advantages and utilities, or hurts. A sheep, for example, when it sees a wolf coming, flees from it as from a natural enemy, and not on account of any unseemliness in the wolf's colour or shape. And in the same way a bird collects straw, not because this is delightful to sense, but because it is useful for nest building. So it is necessary for an animal to perceive appearances [*intentiones*] of this sort which are not perceived by outer sense.... As regards sensible forms, there is no difference between men and other animals: they are worked on in the same way by external sensibles. But there is a difference as regards the appearances just mentioned; for other animals perceive appearances of this sort only by a kind of natural instinct, whereas man uses also a power of comparison.

Here the Latin verb *percipere*, which I have translated literally by 'perceive', is used according to its etymology with the general sense of 'apprehend' or 'grasp', and in the first passage sense perception is treated as a special variety of apprehension in which the soul may be said to grasp the forms of external things, and even to grasp them directly, when they produce *intentiones*, or representations, of themselves in it. Later, indeed, animals are said to have a faculty other than sense by which they perceive *intentiones* of usefulness and harmfulness. But the peculiar talk of perceiving *intentiones* into which St Thomas falls here seems to have been suggested to him by the peculiarity of the mental occurrence we call seeing a thing as useful or harmful.

During the hundred years in which Descartes, Locke, Berkeley, and Hume played havoc with philosophical terminology the word 'perception', like many others, ceased to have any clear meaning, so that in the end Hume thought himself entitled to use it as an omnibus word for whatever goes on in a mind. But in 1764 Reid made an attempt to rescue it, when he wrote in his *Inquiry into the Human Mind*, VI, xx:

Sensation and the perception of external objects by the senses, though very different in their nature, have commonly been considered as one and the same thing. The purposes of common life do not make it necessary to distinguish them, and the received opinion of philosophers tends rather to confound them, but without attending carefully to this distinction it is impossible to have any just conception of the operations of our senses ... Perception, as we here understand it, hath always an object distinct from the act by which it is perceived, an object which may exist whether it be perceived or not ... [Perception] of an object implies both a conception of its form and a belief of its present existence.... I am aware that this belief which I have in perception stands exposed to the strongest batteries of scepticism. But they make no great impression on it.

In the next section, where he considers the causal processes leading up to sensation and perception, he summarizes his conclusions as follows:

Thus our perception of objects is the result of a train of operations, some of which affect the body, others affect the mind.... We know very little of the nature of some of these operations or in what way they contribute to that perception which is the result of the whole, but by the laws of our constitution we perceive objects in this and in no other way.

Obviously Reid is right in trying to rescue the word 'perceive' from misuse. He is right also in two of his detailed theses – namely, first, that the word should be reserved for cases of seeing, hearing, smelling, feeling, and tasting in which the object perceived is independent of its being perceived, and second, that perception, so understood, necessarily involves sensation caused by the object of the perception. These are in accordance with the analyses of older philosophers such as St Thomas, and it is clear that, if we did not already have the word 'perception' for the role they indicate, we should have to invent another with the same meaning. On the other hand, he goes wrong when he suggests that a perception differs from its sensation by the addition of an irresistible belief in the existence of an external cause of that sensation. Certainly anyone who makes a sincere statement to the effect that he perceives something must have a belief about the causation of a sensation. But the belief is required for the sincerity of the statement, not for the perception. This is evident to me from consideration of a curious experience I had many years ago, and I think it will be equally evident to anyone who finds my story intelligible.

I had a heavy cold with a feverish headache and was sitting in my college room, wondering whether I ought to put off a pupil I had arranged to see that evening, when suddenly I heard an insistent high-pitched whistle. In my anxious and depressed state I immediately jumped to the conclusion that the noise was, as we sometimes say, in my head. That is to say, I did not believe that my auditory sensation was caused by any event occurring at the time outside my body and so did not believe that I was hearing a sound in the ordinary sense in which a sound is a common perceptible object. Convinced now that duty and interest both required me to put off the tutorial, I decided to send a message to my pupil, but before I could rise to go to the telephone my servant opened the door of the room and as he did so the sound became louder. At this I jumped to a new and reassuring conviction that my sense experience was due to an external cause, and when I asked my servant what was happening he filled in the detail by telling me that something had gone wrong with the gas ring on the landing outside my door. Surely it was then correct for me to say in retrospect that what I heard during the period of a few seconds in which I thought I had some fault in my hearing was really a common perceptible sound? But if so, it cannot also be correct to say that perception involves acquisition of a belief. For though I did in fact acquire a belief about the origin of my auditory sensation before the door was opened, this was not only false but of a kind not thought necessary for perception by Reid or any other philosopher, and I disregarded it when I decided later that my experience had after all been perception.

When dealing with the cases A-D in Section III of his paper, Roxbee Cox admits that people may sometimes be said correctly to see, feel or hear independent objects though they have no true beliefs of the sort he requires in his analysis of perception, but he suggests that use of perception words to describe such cases is parasitic on their use in the cases he considers normal. It is, of course, true that we take as standard the cases in which we are satisfied at the time of perception that we perceive something; but that is because we are language users for whom learning to use perception words involved essentially learning to apply them to incidents in our own lives. Without that basis we could have no confidence in any other application, but it does not follow that in other applications we normally ascribe beliefs possible only for language users such as we are, and the cases **A-D**, which Roxbee Cox mentions as apparent counter-examples to his thesis, are indeed genuine counter-examples. In each of them, as in the story I have told, a language user is said to perceive something though he raises a question or forms a belief of a kind possible only for a language user but not possible for a perceiver according to Roxbee Cox's analysis of perception. From the fact that perception words are applied in such cases it is reasonable to conclude that they may also be applied in the same sense to animals without language – if indeed any proof is needed for this thesis.

Roxbee Cox does not follow Reid in saying explicitly that a man who perceives something has a correct belief about the cause of a sensation. But I cannot understand why he supposes that his story has anything to do with what older philosophers called *sense* perception unless I am allowed to assume that the letter '*s*' in condition DP(v) of his analysis may be taken as an abbreviation for 'involving production of a certain sense experience'. In his own comment on the passage he goes so far as to suggest that '*s*' may perhaps be equivalent to 'involving [a certain] experience', but he then sheers away from the subject rapidly as though he does not want to admit that perception has any necessary connection with sensation, and I suspect that dislike for talk of sense experience may be one of his motives for trying to analyse perception in terms of the causation of beliefs. However that may be, his final account is notably more complex than that of Reid and therefore more obviously inapplicable to the perception of animals without language. In particular, his condition DP(vi) is one that cannot be fulfilled by such animals, because it requires use of the probabilistic notion of general reliability, a notion that involves in turn the concept of a proposition. He himself is aware of the difficulty and therefore concedes at the end of the third part of his paper that perception may perhaps be said to occur whenever a belief in a state of affairs is caused by that state of affairs. Lacking, as it does, any reference to sense experience, the simple new definition is in one way too wide, because it covers much that is certainly not perception in any ordinary use of that word, e.g. my recollection that I have just written the word 'word'. But in another way it is still too narrow, because it excludes many quite respectable cases of perception, e.g. my hearing the whistle of a gas ring when I thought I heard only 'noises in the head'.

In my opinion the only way out of such troubles is to give up completely the suggestion that perception involves belief. No doubt whenever anyone perceives anything he is in a state apt for the formation of beliefs, should his attention be directed that way. That is why we readily ascribe beliefs of an appropriate kind to people when their perceptions are mentioned in explanation of their behaviour. If, for example, it is said that a woman heard a child crying and went to comfort it, we assume without question that she thought there was a child in distress near by. But it is a mistake (unfortunately common in our time) to identify the *meaning* of a word with the *point* of using it in a certain situation. When our task is to elucidate meanings, we should always hold to the Principle of Minimum Commitment, and in a discussion of perception this implies that we should take seriously such uses as 'I must have seen the thing, though I failed to notice it and genuinely believed it was not there'. For a person who starts with the assumptions of Reid and Roxbee Cox, a remark of this kind must seem very paradoxical. But if we are prepared to admit it as a genuine example of the basic sense of 'see', we can understand all the other uses without difficulty, and in particular we can appreciate why mistakes in the formation of perceptual beliefs are commonly described by phrases like 'he thought he saw', rather than by locutions such as 'he mis-saw'. There are indeed some rather curious cases in which we talk of mis-reading and mis-hearing, but these are concerned with mistakes of recognition and therefore lend no support to a suggestion that perception itself may properly be contrasted with something mistaken, as it might be if it involved true belief or the acquisition of such.

When a true belief that-p arises directly from perception, acquisition of the belief may be described as perceiving-that-p. Roxbee Cox leans heavily on this fact when constructing his general theory of perception. But it is certainly not true that all respectable talk of perceiving can be reduced to talk of perceiving-that, and even in cases where such reduction seems at first glance to be feasible further reflection shows that simple perception is more basic. If I take my coat to a valeting shop for repair of a hole and the manager tells me 'No one will be able to see the darn', he intends, of course, to convey that no one will be able to discern the area of damage and see that it has been darned. But he certainly does not mean that this result will be achieved by use of invisible wool. For if persons who see my coat after the repair fail to see that part of it has been darned, this can only be because the darned part *looks* like the rest. And to say that the darned part escapes notice by looking like the rest is only to say in another way that people *see* it without discerning it from its background.

II

Should we then revert to the doctrine elaborated by St Thomas from the work of Aristotle and say that to perceive X it to have a sense experience representative of X and caused by X, where X is something external to the body? The question is about ordinary language; for although the verb 'perceive' has always been much less common in daily life than in the writings of philosophers and psychologists, it is for these, as Roxbee Cox says, no more than a general term intended to cover the ordinary uses of 'see', 'feel', 'hear', etc., and so our question is really one about the meanings of common words. Although I think St Thomas's definition of perception is a better starting point than that of Reid, I find it unsatisfactory in four respects, and I think that statement of my criticisms may perhaps be the best way in which I can contribute to the discussion.

In the first place St Thomas's account is too narrow, because it assumes the externality of all objects of perception and therefore requires us to say that no one can perceive any part of his body except by feeling or seeing it as something external to another part that serves as organ of perception. In fact one of our most important modes of perception is that by which we feel the relative positions and the relative movements of the parts of our body from within. Because it has no easily identified organs, and also because it provides the basis of reference for all the rest, it has been ignored in traditional lists of the senses, but without it we should lack all power of purposive movement and in particular all power of perceptual exploration by the movement of our sense organs.

Since the seventeenth century, philosophers who write of perception have commonly used the word 'external' with the special sense of 'external to the mind' or 'independently existing', and it may be that when St Thomas spoke about external causes of sense experience he wished already to convey that meaning. For in his usage and that of other medieval philosophers the faculty called internal sense is concerned solely with inner life in the metaphorical sense of that phrase (e.g. with memory, imagination, judgement) and is therefore not at all like the internal perception of which I have spoken. In my view the distinction of mental and physical is one that can be made only by animals that communicate by use of language; but if I am right, there is no good reason to doubt that an animal that lacks language may distinguish between itself and the rest of the world in the way presupposed by an ordinary description of animal behaviour such as 'The cat tried to catch the mouse'. For we ourselves can find a difference between internal and external in our perceptual life. No doubt there is something appropriate in talk of the mental as internal, since otherwise such talk would be unintelligible; but we shall fall into dangerous confusion if we fail to realize that it is only a metaphor derived from another contrast in which 'internal' and 'external' have their original sense.

Secondly, what St Thomas says about sense experience seems to me misleading. It is true he does not use any words corresponding exactly to the English phrase 'sense experience', but I think it is clearly such experience he is talking about when he says that the operation of sense leads to a change in the soul with production of an *intentio*. In my translation of the passage I used 'appearance' as a rendering for *intentio*, because I wanted a word that might be used again later with some plausibility in translation of his remarks about seeing

74

things as useful or harmful. In other places St Thomas himself says that an *intentio* is a *similitudo*, or likeness, of something, and I am afraid that what he wants to convey by using the word here is what Descartes and Locke try to convey by talking of ideas of sense. In other words, he is committed to the view that for sensation as well as for thought the soul must have in it entities with a purely representative status. Aristotle had said that in each case the soul received into itself the forms of things without their matter, but his medieval followers realized that this could not be taken literally, and they did their best to make sense of it by saying that what the soul contained were *species intentionales*, that is to say, representative forms or appearances. At the Renaissance, when Platonic language was fashionable, these were renamed ideas, and from that time until this century discussion of them dominated philosophy with the disastrous effects of which we are now aware. Possibly St Thomas thought that, if an *intentio* of the external cause were formed in a man's soul during sense experience, it would be able to serve as the required conception of the cause when the man came to believe in the existence of the cause. If so, he was preparing the way for the sort of theory we have found in Reid, but I do not regard that as a recommendation for his work.

There are at least some kinds of sense experience, in particular seeing, hearing and smelling, which may be said to have dependent objects, but these latter are not to be confused with *intentiones* nor yet with what we sometimes call in modern times intentional objects – that is, objects of thought. When I mistakenly assumed that my hearing had been affected by a heavy cold, I believed for the moment that my worrying experience was not perception of a common perceptible sound, but I had no doubt that it could be described properly as hearing something, provided only the words 'hearing something' were used in a reduced sense, i.e. without the implication that what I heard might be heard by others or recorded by a machine. Obviously my ability to conceive this reduced sense depended on my being a language user; for an animal without a language can have no notion of perception and therefore no notion of sensation-that-falls-short-of-perception. No doubt such an animal may sometimes have sensations that are not perceptions, but it is absurd to suppose that when this occurs he must be able to meditate wordlessly on the questions about sense-data that worried G. E. Moore. If, then, an animal has a sense experience such as I, a language user, would find it natural to describe by saying that it involved a dependent object, what is necessary to make the experience a perception is not that its dependent object be an idea of the cause of the experience (which is not even possible), but simply that this dependent object *represent* the cause of the experience in the way in which any individual effect may be said to represent its individual cause, i.e. by exhibiting special features that are explicable in the circumstances only by reference to special features of the cause. When a naturalist says that a hole in the ground shows marks of a badger's occupation, or an art historian says that a picture shows traits characteristic of Vermeer's workmanship, he has this notion of representation in mind. It is a commonplace of ordinary human thinking and appropriate here not only for that reason but also because animals without language, who cannot acquire the notion, may nevertheless react to representations of this kind in an instinctive way and even learn new patterns of behaviour under their guidance.

Someone may perhaps object that, while my account of the matter does not require animals without language to think of a relation of sensory representation, it does require such thinking by human beings and must for that reason be condemned, since human beings, who talk of perception, are in no better position than dumb animals for comparing a sensory representation with its original. This is a version of the criticism usually considered fatal to theories of representative perception, but I do not think it need worry me, because I am not committed to the thesis that anyone perceives, or even might perceive, things in a non-sensory way in order to determine that they are really like the sensory representations through which I say they are ordinarily perceived. The representation I require need not involve similarity in any ordinary sense, and our learning of the use of perception words is not an excursion behind the veil of sense, but a piece of animal learning of the kind I noticed a moment ago, though one that requires a more complicated learning mechanism than most animals possess. When through cooperation we have made the great gain of establishing a language, we have freed ourselves in two ways from the limitations of sense. As individuals we can now, if necessary, make good some of the defects of our own sensory equipment by calling on the help of others; and as a race we can make a beginning of natural science by formulating hypotheses about the independent physical world of which we get a conception through the comparisons made possible by conversation. As Cicero said in a different context, 'Our superiority over the beasts consists solely, or chiefly, in the fact that we talk to one another.'

The third criticism I have to bring against St Thomas's account of sense perception is more difficult to explain and I cannot deal with it here in detail, though I must say something about it. Like many other philosophers, St Thomas writes of sense perception as though we received representations of things one by one and perceived in the same way everything of which we received a representation. In fact any representation with a spatial or temporal pattern appears within a sense field possessing what Ward called extensity and protensity. I cannot see a building without seeing something of a fairly complex structure that stands out against a background, and this is as much as to say that I cannot receive a representation of a building without receiving both representations of things that are its parts and representations of things that are not its parts. Similarly, in order to hear a characteristic bird song I must hear a number of distinguishable sounds punctuated by intervals of relative quiet. Now in certain circumstances I may say correctly that I must have seen all the visible parts of a building, i.e. must have received representations of them, though I have not seen the building as a whole because I did not descry it, that is to say, did not discern it from its background. It is indeed just this sort of result that camouflage experts try to bring about by colouring parts of buildings in irregular ways so that the straight lines of the complete structure will not stand out against the fields. In academic circles the contrast of figure and ground has been a favourite topic of

Gestalt psychologists for many years, and more recently Gilbert Ryle has written of perception as though he thought seeing, hearing, feeling, and the rest were always achievements of discernment. The subject is complicated, and I shall only try to make two points about it.

Although we often try to discern things, in particular when we make a search for something of a certain description which we could give in detail, it is by no means the case that all discernment comes as the result of searching or active observation. A flash of lightning in a dark sky will catch my attention whether or not I am looking for one; so, too, will anything that moves fairly fast within my field of view, or anything that stands well forward from its background. Among sounds I am more likely to discern human speech than random squeaks of the same loudness. Undoubtedly searching helps sometimes: everyone knows that he must make an effort to find a pin that has fallen on the floor or to catch the words of his neighbour at a noisy sherry party. But it is only an occasional condition for discernment, i.e. neither necessary nor sufficient in all circumstances. Perhaps Ryle overestimated its importance because he began his inquiry with the conviction that having a mind is simply being able to behave intelligently. In reality intelligence presupposes sentience, and discernment is primarily an affair of sentience, though it may involve a great deal of activity by the sentient organism. In vision, for example, discernment of objects close at hand seems to depend on rapid eye movements, for making which we have an innate behaviour pattern, as anyone may prove to himself by trying to stare at a point without allowing his eyes to do any random scanning.

Because discernment of a thing is necessary for recognition of it as a specimen of a kind and, conversely, recognition of a thing as a specimen of a kind is necessary for success in an attempt to discern it, the two have often been confused. But discernment can occur with no more recognition than is involved in a feeling of surprise, as when for example we hear a sudden loud noise. And recognition may take many different forms, while discernment seems to have no varieties. At the bottom of the scale of recognition we have what St Thomas meant when he said that animals perceive the usefulness or harmfulness of certain things by a sort of instinct. It has been shown by experimental ethologists that young birds can be thrown into a panic by the appearance above them of any object similar in outline to a predator, even though they have never seen such a predator. At or near the other end of the scale is the achievement of the physicist who recognizes the track of a new fundamental particle in a cloud chamber because he has worked out in advance what sorts of tracks should be left by particles of different characteristics.

Finally, I want to say something about St Thomas's treatment of perceptual recognition, which has for an intellectual variety the perceiving-that discussed by Roxbee Cox. If in St Thomas's example a sheep sees a wolf coming and flees from it as from a natural enemy, it is quite natural to say that she recognizes the approaching object as dangerous, and it is permissible, though a little less natural, to say she sees that it is dangerous. Our reason for hesitating slightly about the second form of words is simply that it seems more appropriate for talking about human beings who can formulate propositions in words. We do not wish, however, to say that it is quite unsuitable for application to animals, because we apply it quite freely to ourselves in respect of parts of our lives that are lived at a non-verbal level. When a batsman has successfuly played a difficult ball at cricket, he may say 'I saw that it was going to rise', though it is almost certain he did not formulate the thought in words before raising his bat. In such circumstances the words that the man uses after the event are, so to say, a verbal translation of a thought originally expressed in action; and the same holds for what we say about the sheep. But whether we speak of recognizing X as Y or of perceiving that X is Y, we convey more by our language than simple psychological description. To say that a sheep recognizes an approaching wolf as dangerous is to assert (*a*) that the sheep takes the wolf for dangerous and (*b*) that she is right in so doing. Unfortunately, St Thomas seems to overlook this complication when he says that the sheep perceives the harmfulness of the wolf by a sort of instinct. For while it may be true that sheep instinctively take approaching wolves for dangerous, it is also true that they often take harmless things for dangerous, and so it is going too far to say that they perceive harmfulness by instinct, unless one makes clear that such perceiving is quite different from the perceiving of colour by sense in as much as it has an opposite we might call mis-perceiving.

I have the impression that, when Roxbee Cox tries to analyse perceiving in terms of perceiving-that, he falls into the opposite error. It is true that, just as there must be an X if a man sees an X, so there must be an X before a man if he sees that there is an X before him. But in the first case there need be no belief at all, whereas in the second case belief is of the essence of the situation, and when there is belief there might conceivably be false belief. I suppose the old adage 'Seeing is believing' means that some beliefs of the sort a man might express by saying 'I see that there is an X before me' are, as Reid held, irresistible. And this I am prepared to concede. But simple seeing is certainly not believing, nor yet coming to believe, since it is just not the sort of thing that could conceivably be mistaken – or right either.

Analysing Seeing

I

F. N. SIBLEY

I

Certain accounts of perception, particularly some recent ones, may be seen by an admitted simplification as developing or defending one or other of two opposing positions. Since these accounts often give major consideration to seeing, I too shall follow this not altogether happy tradition.

These opposing accounts both concern not what is seen but seeing itself, that capacity and its exercise which the non-blind have and the blind lack. The accounts may conveniently, if not very accurately, be labelled respectively 'epistemic' and 'non-epistemic'. The former attempts to analyse seeing (or perception generally) in terms of belief (or knowledge) or the acquisition of beliefs. According to it, an analysis of seeing things or events necessarily involves reference to believing-that, or to seeing-that, which in turn is analysed, partially at least, in terms of believing-that. It is not held, generally, that seeing-that can occur without seeing things or events; but it is held that the former notion is the fundamental one. One, but not the only, impetus to developing this kind of theory is the wish to avoid, and the supposition that only thus can one avoid, the admission of items (sense-data, etc.) that, while analogous to things in having their own visual properties, are not physical or public items but are nevertheless 'perceived' or 'sensed' when we perceive physical things and events.

The opposing account holds that there is some basic seeing (or perceiving) that is 'non-epistemic', i.e. does not necessarily involve acquisition of beliefs (or knowledge) and can be adequately analysed without reference to the concept of belief at all. On this view, although someone who sees a thing or event may also in fact see-that something, and so acquire some belief,

81

the notion of seeing-that must be analysed by reference to the more basic and non-epistemic notion, seeing. Certain words of Warnock's are sometimes referred to with approval by holders of this position: 'If there is a sense, as there is, in which we speak of the ability to see as a physical capacity, in which being able to see better than others is not to enjoy any superiority of wits, skill, talent or experience, then there must be a sense in which seeing does not involve the acquired abilities to identify, recognize, name, describe, and so on' (Warnock, p. 65).[1] Strictly, these words do not support a non-epistemic position since Warnock does not explicitly mention *belief*, but only identifying, recognizing, etc.; as far as this quotation goes, the basic kind of seeing might necessarily involve the acquiring of beliefs, but not recognizing, identifying, or any of the other abilities mentioned. Nevertheless, rightly or wrongly, mention of a *physical* capacity, and the implied non-necessity of wits, etc., suggest a kind of seeing from which all mental, or more than physical, capacities and achievements may be lacking, and, *a fortiori*, a non-epistemic kind of seeing (certainly other things Warnock says have a similar tendency, e.g. one might see without making or being able to make 'any judgment at all' (p. 52)).

In this paper I do not undertake to develop or defend any systematic analysis of seeing of either kind. I confess I have hitherto supposed a non-epistemic account possible, but the issue now seems to me more complex and obscure. Certainly a satisfactory account of seeing that shows it to be entirely non-epistemic has yet to be given, and I have doubts whether such is possible. On the other hand, while belief-analyses, as sometimes developed, embody errors that can be fairly convincingly exposed, it has yet to be shown that a modestly epistemic account of the basic notion of seeing is not necessary or tenable. What I attempt, therefore, is to set out considerations that seem to favour an epistemic view and present difficulties for the contrary view. They may make it, I suggest, not unreasonable to suppose that any adequate account of seeing must involve or make reference to the acquiring of beliefs, and so to the concept of belief; or, at the very least, they may make clearer what has to be rejected if an epistemic account is to be ruled out and an entirely non-epistemic account established.

To this preamble I add five further comments. First, I try, though this is not altogether possible, to avoid direct discussion of others' views, for instance Dretske's[2] and Armstrong's,[3] even though these may constitute the best or most typical accounts of the opposing views to date. Secondly, I aim throughout to bear in mind seeing as it occurs, or may naturally be assumed to occur, in animals and infants as well as in adults. Thirdly, I am concerned with cases where what are seen are objects, events and other publicly visible phenomena, like shadows, changes of lighting or foreign bodies in the eye, *not* with cases of hallucination. Fourthly, I want, like most of those on each side of the epistemic/non-epistemic dispute (including both Armstrong and Dretske), to deal with these bona fide and non-hallucinatory cases of seeing without introducing any additional non-physical (but coloured, etc.) items (sense-data, or whatever). Finally, it should be said here, there is one respect in which I am not engaging in the epistemic/non-epistemic debate. Usually this takes the form of a dispute over whether, to put it roughly, it is seeing (with direct object) or seeing-that (agreed on all hands to be epistemic) which is the primary or more fundamental notion. Dretske, for instance, argues that the former, which he takes to be non-epistemic, is the more fundamental, while Armstrong apparently takes the opposite position (the 'information-flow' account of perception can 'explain the other idiom', p. 228). In the present paper, however, seeing-that, which is clearly epistemic, is not discussed; nor is it denied that seeing is more fundamental than seeing-that. Rather it is proposed that there are two (visual) uses of 'see' with direct object, one epistemic, one not, and that the epistemic is in various respects the more fundamental. A totally non-epistemic account of seeing, on the other hand, will be one, whether or not it allows that there are epistemic as well as non-epistemic uses of 'see' with direct object, that holds that it is a non-epistemic use of 'see' that is fundamental.

II

I now need to explain more fully the labels I am using. An 'epistemic' account asserts that the basic use of 'see' is such that, if S sees D, S necessarily thereby or therein acquires *some belief or other*. Following the lines laid down by others on both sides of the present dispute, I apply the term 'belief' to animals, infants, etc. ('The beliefs involved must be conceived as subverbal beliefs. Animals can perceive sometimes, we believe, better than we can, but they lack words entirely.' We attribute beliefs to them on the basis of their 'as-if believing' behaviour though, admittedly, 'to talk of beliefs may seem to be to talk in a very sophisticated and self-conscious way' (Armstrong, p. 209). 'As I am using this term ["belief"], a person (or animal) may know that something is the case and believe it' (Dretske, p. 6).) There are also questions about the propriety of speaking of *acquiring* beliefs, given that when S sees or continues to see D he may already have the belief in question; again I will follow Armstrong who speaks here (p. 214) of acquiring 'new, even if monotonous' beliefs. By a 'non-epistemic' account I mean one that asserts that the basic use of 'see' is such that S can see D without acquiring *any belief at all*. Various more detailed positions can be sketched however. For instance, the view that if S sees D there is no *particular* belief that he must acquire is compatible with an epistemic or a non-epistemic account as defined above. If it means that S must acquire some, though no particular, belief, it might be called a 'broadly epistemic' account and contrasted with a 'specific epistemic' account, namely, that to see D, S must acquire some particular or specific belief. I think this last view (which is explicitly attacked by Dretske) clearly untenable, though I am not sure whether any recent philosophers have held it. Other epistemic views, however, could be held: e.g. that if S sees D, S must acquire some, but no particular belief, but one of some particular and specifiable *kind*; it may be this sort of view that Armstrong holds. I shall argue later that, even if it is true that S must acquire some belief or other, and even perhaps of a particular kind, it need not be of the kind that Armstrong, for instance, seems to suggest. It is also worth noting at this point, as an addition to what I have said, that there may be some uses of 'see' such that S's seeing D does not necessarily involve S's acquiring any belief; these might be called 'non-epistemic' uses to contrast with those 'epistemic' uses in which acquisition of belief is an essential element. I shall have this alternative application of 'non-epistemic' and 'epistemic' to *uses* in mind throughout, even though such a 'non-epistemic' use of 'seeing' might still reasonably be regarded as ultimately epistemic if an account or elucidation of it had necessarily to make reference to or employ an epistemic use of 'seeing' (and therefore also the concept of belief).

I have indicated that both Warnock and Dretske might be supposed to be committing themselves to what I am calling non-epistemic accounts of seeing. Whether this supposition is correct is something I want to consider a little further. Dretske certainly claims that the basic use of 'see' (what he calls 'seeing$_n$') is non-epistemic; but from many of his statements and examples (pp. 5-17) it does not follow that his account is non-epistemic in my sense at all. What he repeatedly denies is that, if S sees D, there is some *particular* belief that S must thereby have or acquire; and this, which is compatible with what I called a 'broadly epistemic' view, may be all he intends. On the other hand, some of his statements could bear either interpretation, and at least one suggests the more extreme position ('I, personally, have no idea what the infant or the rat believes, *or whether they believe anything*', p. 10, my italics). Moreover, in those passages where he offers his positive account of seeing$_n$ (p.18 ff.), there is no suggestion that S must, in seeing D, acquire some belief. And since this account of 'seeing$_n$' is offered, I believe, as a full, not a partial, positive account (he speaks of 'an equivalence', uses an 'equals' sign and so on), we may conclude, I think, that his positive account of seeing *is* totally non-epistemic.

Assuming this, I want to draw attention to what seems to be one necessary condition for seeing, even on a totally non-epistemic theory. This is that, if S sees D at time t, then D *must look somehow to S at t*, a condition stated explicitly by Dretske (p. 20) and indeed used by him to explain seeing$_n$.

But this condition can form part of a non-epistemic account of seeing only if it itself is interpreted as entailing nothing as to whether S thereby acquires a belief. This is presumably what Dretske intends when he explains that the way in which 'look' is here used is one which 'presupposes or entails nothing about whether S *notices* D ... or whether he exploits his visual experience in any way whatsoever' (p. 21, my italics). He stresses this repeatedly, e.g. 'It is a sense of the term "look" in which one might say of S, "He did not notice D, but judging from the conditions he was in, and the direction he was looking, it is likely that D *looked some way* to him"' (p. 21). Warnock similarly seems to imply that some such condition is logically necessary for seeing, though he uses the word 'appears' instead of 'looks' (e.g. 'it is a mistake to suppose that seeing things essentially involves knowing, or getting to know, what they are, or what they are like, *or even how they appear*', p. 53, my italics). Dretske glosses his condition by saying that 'D occupies a portion of S's visual field', and Warnock says, rather similarly, that 'one who sees must have a field of vision, and that what he may rightly be said to see must be in it' (p. 53). So I shall take it that this condition, as glossed above, is held by some writers to be a necessary condition of S's seeing D. Equally I assume that, for a totally non-epistemic account of seeing, which I am attributing to Dretske, the expressions 'D looks somehow to S' and 'D is in S's visual field' must themselves be totally non-epistemic; that is, not only do they not presuppose or entail that S *notices* D (or even how D looks) – the view explicitly held by Dretske and also apparently by Warnock – but they also presuppose or entail nothing about S's acquiring any *belief*.

There is a reason for thus distinguishing *noticing* and acquiring *beliefs*. It is presumably plausible enough to hold (1) that noticing (or becoming aware or conscious of) D entails acquiring some belief or other. There is also a temptation, discussed by Warnock, to think (2) that if S saw D, S must have noticed, or become aware or conscious of D. But (1) and (2) together entail what we are interested in, (3), that for S to see D, S must acquire some belief or other. It is worth asking therefore whether the temptation to hold that (3) is true results simply from an inclination to accept the tempting view (2) (e.g. that 'if Jones sees a fox, he must at least be conscious of a – perhaps to him unidentified and unconsidered – *something* in his field of vision; if not, it must surely be absurd to say that he sees it'), a view that Warnock rejects (pp. 54-8). He rejects it, however, in a somewhat tentative way (e.g. 'indeed one might say that for most of us there is, about most of the things that we see, simply nothing to notice (*particularly*)' (p. 54, my italics), and 'It may be that in some sense – which deserves more consideration than I have given it – it must be true that A was conscious of X; however, there is certainly *a* sense in which this is not necessary' (p. 58)), which leaves the present question still in the air. For first, even if expressions like 'notice', 'conscious of', etc., *often* bear *specialized* senses making it inappropriate to apply one of them to any and every case of seeing, it is still, as Warnock half-admits, possible that there may be other senses of these expressions such that some one of them (and perhaps indeed one implying beliefs) is always applicable. One may continue to feel, perhaps rightly, that if D looked somehow to S but S did not *in any sense* notice, or was not *in some sense* aware of, or did not give *any* attention to D, etc., then S did not see D. That is, one may continue to be troubled by one side of Warnock's apparent dilemma (p. 55): 'seeing is in peril of becoming attenuated to the object's merely being before his eyes; it is however a mere physical fact that this is so, and it is rightly felt that seeing must amount to more than this'. Warnock thinks we are perhaps tempted here to 'sponsor' an invented use of expressions like 'notice', 'conscious of', etc., 'such that it is to be simply analytic that what one sees one is conscious of'. One might counter, equally tentatively, that we need not sponsor, since we already have, in our normal speech about perception, non-specialized and analytic uses of these locutions by which we often replace 'see' precisely when we wish to stress that actual seeing (and hence the belief-acquisition that these locutions imply), and not mere physical presence before the eyes, was what occurred. But secondly, even if 'non-specialized' or 'analytic' uses of these expressions do not exist, it is still conceivable that (3) above is true. One needs still to investigate whether, for S to see D, (in addition to D's looking somehow to S in a sense that does not imply S's noticing D, and even if it *is* inappropriate to employ such words as 'notice') S must also have acquired some belief. For instance, if, as seems plausible, paying some degree of attention to something entails acquiring at least some belief, and if one cannot be said to see D without paying at least some minimal attention to D, seeing will necessarily involve acquiring some belief. Whatever the intentions of Warnock's article, his words do not explicitly deny, any more than his arguments disprove, that seeing may be ultimately epistemic.

III

I shall now take it that a totally non-epistemic account of seeing maintains that there is a basic use of 'see' ('see$_n$') the analysis of which does not involve reference to the notions of belief or acquiring beliefs (I shall assume that Dretske's is such an account). The primary question is whether such an account is correct. I shall take it also that if S sees D, D looks somehow to S in a sense that does not entail any acquisition of belief by S; indeed, this use of 'looks' must also be totally non-epistemic. I shall therefore use the expression 'looking$_n$', and assume this is Dretske's sense.

For a non-epistemic account of seeing, as for Dretske's, the positive characterization of 'seeing$_n$' (which 'has no belief content') will be in terms of 'looking$_n$' (cf. Dretske, pp. 19-20). I shall allow myself to say that, for such an account, from 'D looks$_n$ somehow to S' the truth of 'S sees$_n$ D' would follow, and indeed that the two expressions would be equivalent. Strictly, for Dretske this is not so. D's looking somehow to S is a necessary, but not a sufficient, condition for S's seeing$_n$ D (p. 24); his further condition is that what is seen$_n$ must 'appear to one as a more or less differentiated part' of what one sees. His equivalence is thus that for S to see$_n$ D, D must, in addition to looking somehow to S, be 'visually differentiated from its immediate environment by S' (p. 20), where this presumably does not imply that S *differentiates* D from its environment (which would surely imply noticing D and therefore acquiring some belief or other), but only that D must be *capable* of being *differentiated* from its environment by S.

Nevertheless, apart from this differentiation clause (which I discuss later), 'D looks$_n$ somehow to S' and 'S sees$_n$ D' would be equivalent; so I shall for the moment treat them as such and speak of their *virtual* equivalence. Since the core of the analysis or characterization of 'seeing$_n$' is, for a non-epistemic account, in terms of 'looking$_n$' we need to ask two questions about them both: (1) Are they familiar notions, ones we use and understand? and (2) Are they, as both must be, not only non-epistemic, but also basic; that is, can an intelligible account be given of them without any reference to belief or some other epistemic notion? The reply to the first question is, I think, that non-epistemic uses of the verbs 'look' and 'see' quickly turn out to be familiar enough. The reply to the second question is less straightforward.

But first, at the risk of tedium and to forestall possible confusions, I want to clarify further the use of 'looks$_n$' (and of 'seems$_n$' or 'appears$_n$') needed in this discussion. First, in all uses of 'looks' that concern me, 'looks' functions as a *sense-indicator*, i.e. it indicates a connection with *vision*, just as 'smells' or 'sounds' indicate connections with other specific senses (whereas 'seems' and 'appears', though often used in connection with vision, do not necessarily indicate one sense rather than another). Secondly, I say nothing about that use of 'looks' in which, besides being a sense-indicator, it is also an (often firm but sometimes tentative) *opinion-indicator* about how something *is*, e.g. as in some uses of 'she looks exhausted'. (I similarly ignore uses of 'seems' and 'appears' which are (firm or tentative) opinion-indicators about how something *is*, as in some uses of e.g. 'the plank seems rotten'.) These are ways of saying that one thinks (or is inclined to think), from the way she looks, that she *is* exhausted (or from something or other, perhaps sight, perhaps smell, that the plank *is* rotten). These opinion-indicating uses of 'looks', etc., have had their fair share of attention in recent writing. The only uses of 'looks' that concern me have to do with (visual) *appearances*; those uses, that is, that cover and are inclusive of *both* 'mere' appearances (as when, to the philosopher's delight, a tilted round plate looks elliptical, a distant green mountain looks blue or, even, a cushion doubled up in a chair looks just like a cat asleep) *and* appearances that coincide with what is in fact the case ('red things in normal light look red', 'she not only looks exhausted, she is', 'the thing on the chair that looks like a cat asleep *is* a cat asleep'); that is, I am concerned with a thing's looking ∅ (or like ∅) where this is compatible both with its *being* ∅ and with its *merely* looking ∅. (So, similarly, with 'seems' and 'appears': they may cover both 'it not only seems lower in pitch; it *is*' and 'it only seems lower because it's moving away'.) One recipe (but only a rough one *and not the only one by far*) for providing a description of how a thing, D, looks$_n$ to S that fits this inclusive visual appearance use of 'looks' is to find the descriptions (e.g. 'elliptical' or 'bluish') that would correctly describe what the shape, colour, etc., of marks to be put on a flat upright canvas *really are* if one were attempting a *trompe-l'œil* depiction of D from S's standpoint. It is then correct to say that D *looks$_n$* thus (i.e. elliptical or bluish). But I emphasize that this 'flat canvas' or 'Leonardo's window' description of how D looks$_n$ to S is only one of an indefinitely large number.

It seems to me fairly certain that we often employ 'looks' in the non-epistemic way indicated: that anything which a person, S, sees (or can see) at t looks$_n$ to him somehow at t. It seems clear too that a man to whom D looks$_n$ ∅ may not notice or observe how D looks$_n$ to him, and that when he is asked how something looks$_n$ to him, the answer he gives may be mistaken. When asked how the distant mountains look$_n$ today, I may, after looking at them, give my opinion that they look bluish. But if asked to look again to see whether I am not mistaken, through inattention, prior expectation, etc., and whether today they do not look greyish rather than bluish, I may look again and agree. (This, incidentally, is the only epistemic or opinion-indicating aspect of the use of 'looks' that is of interest in this paper, namely, when a person, being asked how the cushion or the mountains look$_n$ to him, replies by saying, e.g., 'it looks like a cat' or 'they look bluish', and in doing so is giving his opinion about how things *look$_n$* to him. I am not at all concerned with his opinion about how or what a things *is*, but only how it *looks$_n$*.)

I want to specify in one further respect how I am using 'looks$_n$ to him'. In assuming so far that S's eyes are normal, 'to him', in 'D looks$_n$ ∅ to him', functions as a position, lighting and, in general, *physical situation indicator*. 'To him' means 'from where he is, now, at t' (not to someone else at a different angle, or time). Sometimes, however, 'to him' may function additionally to indicate that we are concerned particularly, or also, with how D looks$_n$ to *him* in particular, given the permanent or temporary, and not necessarily normal, condition of his eyes or other physiological apparatus. Here 'to him' is also an *optical condition indicator*. If S has migraine, D may look dislocated or inverted, or if he has jaundice it may look yellow-tinged to him, but not to others who are normal. Often the ophthalmologist's questions or tests are concerned precisely to find out how things look$_n$ in this sense to a given person. Similarly, while to me the E on a test card at a given distance looks to consist simply of upright and horizontal bars, to you, with better eyes, it may look to have serifs in addition. As before, so in these cases too, S's opinion about how D looks$_n$ to him may be mistaken. He may not notice the yellowish tinge until the optician directs his attention thereto.

To summarize, the sense in which D looks$_n$ somehow to S, as I use it, where this is a necessary condition for S's seeing D, concerns D's looking somehow to S independently of whether he notices, half-notices or 'misnotices' it; and whether and how D looks to S in this sense depends on both his physical situation and his physiological condition. How D looks$_n$ to a normal adult human is something he can ordinarily, by paying attention, find out, though it may require care and close attention. (For instance, as I am using 'looks$_n$', an ellipse in fact often looks$_n$ flatter than one supposes; the phenomena of 'size and shape constancy' are concerned, *not* with how things look$_n$, but with how, mistakenly, we are inclined to suppose they look$_n$. However, while it seems to me that 'looks$_n$' must be the notion employed in a non-epistemic account of seeing, Dretske's comment (footnote, p. 23) on the constancies, that 'the percipient's beliefs play a role in the way "things look to him"' implies that the notion I have explained is not in fact his notion.) Having paid appropriate attention, S will then have knowledge, or opinion, true or false, about how D then looks$_n$ to him. What the doctor or optician learns about this is what S, by applying his attention as fully as possible, can report, notice, react to, etc. Students of animal vision learn, though often only by ingenious tests, how things look$_n$ to animals from the non-verbal responses, reactions, etc., they can elicit when the animal has been brought to notice D. We could have no notion of S giving an opinion, correct or mistaken, about how D looked to him without this notion of looking$_n$; and if D does not look$_n$ anyhow to S, D is invisible to him. (Often, of course, a question about how D looks$_n$ to S is not intended in the 'optical-indicative' way here discussed, but only 'situation-indicatively', i.e. to ask how D looks in this light, from that distance and angle, to those with normal vision. Often, rightly understanding the question thus, S can, even if his eyes are defective or affected in certain ways, but provided he knows this, give an answer (possibly correct) about how D looks 'to him'. He would not then, except as a joke, describe how D looked to him while his eyes happened to be watering; nor need the jaundice sufferer, to whom D (which he knows is white but in shadow) looks a yellowish grey, say other than that it looks greyish.)

IV

Given this necessary condition of seeing, that D looks$_n$ somehow to S, S may notice D, and perhaps more or less how D looks$_n$ to him, depending on the degree of attention he pays. It also seems contingently possible for him to fail entirely to notice or to acquire any belief about D or how D looks. A first question is whether, in this second case, S has *seen* D, or whether on the contrary he did not see D but was merely *in a position* or *able* to see D (i.e. he merely had a visual field *available* for his possible attention, in a way the blind do not). A wholly non-epistemic account will presumably hold that this *does* constitute seeing ('seeing$_n$'), and that this use of seeing is the basic one. But before I answer this question, which is about the necessity or otherwise of attention and belief-acquisition in seeing (which I shall call the 'psychological' or 'mental' factors), I want to comment on the *physical* factors that set the limits on what looks$_n$ somehow to S at a given moment, and so, on any account, set the limits to what he sees or is in a position to see.

Whereas under the head *psychological* or *mental*, just mentioned, I include all factors concerning attention in any of its forms (noticing, spotting, taking in, becoming aware or conscious of, having one's attention caught by something, etc.), I group under the head *physical* a great variety of factors that determine what, and how much detail, we are at a given moment capable of seeing (I largely ignore complexities that result from our having two eyes, from their facing forwards, not sideways, etc.). These factors include the direction of the head and of the eyeball in the socket at any given moment, the relative positions of cheeks, forehead and eyes, the optical focus at any particular moment, and individual variations in ability to focus on objects at given distances. They include, too, keenness or acuity of vision, the ability to see details, when optically focused on a particular point, that another person, similarly focused, cannot see; and they include such temporary variations of visual keenness as result from dazzle, watering eyes, etc. There are also other physical variations and abnormalities that might limit a creature's vision; but these suffice for my purpose. All these physical factors affect what details one is capable of seeing at any particular time, and how distinctly or blurrily they may be seen, if at all.

As far as logic goes mental and physical factors are independent of each other; but there are normally contingent connections and interactions, some but not all of which we can with effort overcome. Direction and focus normally shift with shifts of attention; if attention is taken by something near and to one side while one is focusing on something distant and ahead, the eyes are likely to turn to the new object of attention and refocus on it. But with effort we can to some extent prevent this coordination of direction and/or focus with attention. We can deliberately attend to objects towards the periphery of our vision (and to how they then look, blurry, of uniform colour, etc.) without turning our eyes; or, while focusing on the distant trees through the window, attend, without refocusing, to the (blurry) appearance of a scratch on the window pane. What therefore $looks_n$ somehow to S (and how it $looks_n$) is not merely determined at any one moment by the physical factors, but constantly changes from moment to moment because of these complexities (I ignore the further physiological fact that direction of gaze constantly changes by involuntary minute shifts, even when attention is not itself shifting but is concentrated on one detail). The constant rapid changes in both physical and mental factors may lead us into supposing that more can be seen at a given moment than in fact is the case. In what follows, I simplify by imagining all *physical* and *physiological* factors stable for a given moment (I shall refer to such a momentary state as F_1; any change in these factors gives F_2, F_3, etc.). F_1 fixes the limits of what things $look_n$ somehow to S at t. Given such an artificially fixed *physical* and *physiological* situation, I want to consider variations of *mental* condition (e.g. attention) in relation to it.

If, at time t, S is in state F_1, it will be the case, according to a totally non-epistemic use of 'seeing' ('$seeing_n$'), that *everything* that $looks_n$ somehow to S is *actually seen* by S at t (provided only that Dretske's differentiation condition is also added if necessary). On the other hand, with an epistemic use of 'seeing' (I shall call this '$seeing_e$'), only those items are actually seen, amongst all those that at t $look_n$ somehow to S, which S in some degree notices or pays attention to and, in any event, acquires some belief about (which does not suppose that he recognizes, identifies or takes them, correctly or incorrectly, to be this or that). The remainder are merely items in his visual field at t that, while in state F_1, he *could* notice, acquire beliefs about, in short, could or might see_e, by a redirection of attention.

If now we distinguish *focus of attention* from physical or optional focus and direction as determined by F_1, we can consider various cases. First those cases where attention is given to what is not physically focused. If we are physically focused on the trees a hundred feet off, we will ordinarily not notice scratches on the window through which we are looking, even though they are certainly visible to us *at that focus*. We can prove this by noticing them (blurry and unfocused, and, if one is using both eyes, doubly seen) if, while still focusing on the trees, we force our attention to the window pane. (This is obviously to be contrasted with the fact that the *smaller* scratches on the window may be things we could not, with a deliberate shift of attention but unchanged optical focus, notice at all, however fuzzily. At that (distant) focus, F_1, they do not look$_n$ to us anyhow at all.) Again, if by an effort we attend to an object towards the periphery of our visual field while continuing to focus optically on something else in our direct line of vision, we are momentarily capable of not noticing, because our main attention is directed elsewhere, some otherwise perfectly noticeable detail in the optically focused object. Secondly, there are cases where attention, even to whatever is in perfect optical focus, looking$_n$ somehow to us, diminishes or is entirely absent. While listening intently, concentrating on a problem, or daydreaming, our attention may be partly or wholly engaged elsewhere, or engaged nowhere. We no longer notice or are aware of what looks$_n$ somehow to us (for even if, our attention being elsewhere, our eye muscles relax, they are still focused (but now at F_2) on whatever is at the distance of maximum muscle relaxation).

I think it hardly questionable in both sorts of cases, where attention and physical focus diverge and where attention is largely or completely lacking, that even if we allow that certain unnoticed things do look$_n$ somehow to us it is most common to say that whatever we did not notice or give any attention to *we did not see*. In the first kind of case we did not actually see some things that we could then, by shifting our attention but not our focus, have seen; in the second, we saw little or nothing at all, though some things were visible to us and even in focus. We are just as likely to say, normally, that someone does not, or that we did not, actually *see* things, as that we did not *notice* them. Indeed, in such contexts we use the word 'see' interchangeably not only with 'notice' but with such other expressions, all of them implying attention, as 'spot', 'glimpse', 'observe', 'pick out', 'take in', 'note', etc. (No doubt occasions when attention is *totally* distracted from the visible scene while we are awake are rare, if indeed they occur at all. Probably, even when we are 'wholly' distracted, so long as our eyes are open there normally remains, at least for things in the centre of our visual field, about as much of our attention as is ordinarily upon things in the periphery of our visual field. For not only does attention seldom totally lapse; it also, rather like vision, has an area of focus and a penumbra. But, if so, these are largely irrelevant contingent facts.) I am simply urging that as we ordinarily talk, and therefore in a very familiar use of 'see', to say that someone actually saw D, *more* is required than merely that D looked$_n$ somehow to him: the more often being expressed by uses of 'noticed', 'paid attention to', 'caught his attention', 'became conscious of' or others of the expressions mentioned above that imply attention and some acquisition of belief. It is surely beyond dispute that we may not have seen the serifs on the print we have just been reading, even though they were clearly visible to us without alteration of focus or addition of spectacles. We are prepared to say that someone in a brown study, or grief-stricken, or engrossed in argument, 'stared at something unseeing', 'looked right through it, without seeing it', etc. All these are points about our actual use of words; but if they are correct, and if such obviously attention-involving locutions as those listed are interchangeable with 'seeing', it surely cannot be denied that there does exist a use of 'see' that involves attention and hence belief-acquisition. (Just as I take it to be absurd to say that someone glimpsed or spotted or, in one sense, saw something without giving it, or its taking, any of his attention, so I take it as undeniable that someone cannot have spotted or noticed or otherwise given some attention to something without acquiring some belief or other, if only the belief that, e.g., something happened or seemed to. I have said nothing, however, about the content of these beliefs, or of what sort they may or must be if they are to be acquired by *vision*.)[4] If, for example, when a flash occurs, a person does not believe, however momentarily the belief lasts, that something has either occurred or seemed to, he may be said not to have seen the flash. If so, there is one common use of 'see' with direct object that is epistemic (the use I call 'seeing$_e$') in addition to the obviously epistemic uses of 'seeing-

96

that'. By what possible argument could such patent facts of usage be denied?

There are certain arguments that are sometimes offered to show that there exists a common non-epistemic use of 'see', and perhaps, more strongly, that 'see' (with direct object) is not used epistemically. These arguments rest on the fact that where something is directly before a man's eyes, but apparently he did not notice it, we sometimes say, 'he *must* have seen it'. (Dretske uses this fact, p. 19 and elsewhere, to argue that 'see' is used non-epistemically.) I find these arguments wholly inconclusive either *for* an existing non-epistemic use or *against* an existing epistemic one. To the empirical question whether we ever say (as opposed to whether we *must* say), of a creature who seems to have been unaware of its surroundings when its eyes were open, that it 'must have seen them', the answer is surely 'Yes', particularly when the object was large, and in full focus. But the relevant question is what, when we say this, we are committing ourselves to; and this is what remains unclear. It does not seem to me to show that we are thereby committing ourselves to the doctrine that merely having an unnoticed or unattended to visual field constitutes seeing. It seems equally plausible to argue that we are intending to commit ourselves (in so far as we intend anything, or know what we intend), in saying 'S must have seen D', to the view that S must have noticed, acquired some belief about, i.e. seen$_e$, D at the time, however briefly the belief was retained and the episode remembered. If so, our assertion that S must have seen D may often be false; despite being confronted with D, he may not, in the sense we intend, have seen it at all. Equally, the assertion may frequently be true. We might plausibly hold that we often do see$_e$ (notice) things before us, with some slight degree of attention, that we could report something about them an instant later if asked, but that they are of such minimal interest to us, and, as we say, make so little impression, that we retain no memory of them beyond the shortest possible time. This may be so with most of what surrounds us for much of our waking lives. So it seems to me that, in a common use of 'seeing', it may as often be false as true, when people say we must have seen it, that we saw what was before us. We would not necessarily insist that *S*, whom I took into my study for a moment to see the view, *must have seen* the scratches on the window pane as he looked out simply because, since he looked at and focused on the garden and has good eyes, at least the larger scratches looked$_n$ somehow to him. If we insisted even a moment later that he must have seen them, he might often assert flatly that he just had not. Thus again, as far as actual linguistic practice goes, I do not think that we always insist that a man must have seen everything in his visual field. Nor do the *arguments* based on our sometimes saying 'he must have seen *D*' either prove that we do not employ 'see' epistemically or prove the existence of a non-epistemic use of 'see'. To base a conclusion on them seems to be offering a decision on a matter that they fail to decide. Indeed Dretske seems to concede, as far as these arguments go, that one could 'cling to' an epistemic view and either 'continue to insist that I was believing something at the time about the things which I saw' or else insist 'that I really did not see anything' (p. 11). And others in fact do apparently opt this other way. Soltis,[5] for instance, after considering similar arguments says, 'We do treat seeing dominantly as not only the having of visual sensations but also as the *conscious involvement* on the part of the one having those sensations with some object which produces them' (pp. 61-2, my italics); and Quinton[6] (pp. 508-11) appears to have held that having an unnoticed visual field is insufficient to constitute seeing (though he speaks rather of the limited number of 'experiences' of which we are aware being the only ones 'we can be said to perceive'). So there is a difference of opinion over whether seeing is or is not used non-epistemically.

There is one stronger claim made by Dretske – namely, that there is nothing 'logically incoherent' about saying, e.g., 'I must have seen it, but, at the time, I was totally unaware of anything but that pain in my foot' (p. 11). This, if true, presumably entails that a non-epistemic use of 'see' exists, though not, of course, that there is not also the epistemic use I have illustrated and emphasized. Nor does it begin to show, what is at issue, that the non-epistemic use of 'seeing' is more basic than the epistemic.

If now we ask the factual question whether, besides an epistemic use, a non-epistemic use also exists, a glance at linguistic practice seems to show undeniably that it does. People do sometimes, to make a particular kind of point, use 'see$_n$' as well as 'see$_e$'. I think this non-epistemic use is not the most common one; but if it can be illustrated by things people sometimes say, it is not being introduced by a philosopher's decision. It is mainly employed, I think, by those concerned to stress various facts of physiology. In more ordinary contexts it tends to sound outlandish or paradoxical. A typical example from writers on physiology runs thus: 'Consider what happens when you read this page.... You can also see a great deal more than this, though if you are interested in this book, you will not be conscious of it until you take notice.... You can see ... your hands holding the book ... the furniture of the room' (Mann and Pirie, p. 47).[7] (It is equally noteworthy that, within a page, the same writers also employ an apparently epistemic use: 'The Tuatera lizards ... have their eyes at the sides of their heads.... They therefore sacrifice some perception of depth for a larger field of vision with two (instead of one) areas of clear sight in it. *Which they see is a matter of attention*, and that is determined by the relative importance of the two objects to the lizard', p. 48, my italics.) But outside contexts where optical capacities or the extent of a person's visual field at a given moment are being stressed, the non-epistemic use sounds odd. Physiologists may say, to make a point and with deliberate paradox, that a man can see, indeed *actually does* see, the sides of his own nose all the time though without normally noticing them. But though this use doubtless exists, so does the more familiar epistemic one. Consequently it would not be inconsistent to retort that, though the above remarks are in some sense true, a man hardly ever does actually see his own nose. The unfamiliarity of seeing$_n$ would come out if one asked a man whether, while watching cricket, he was also seeing his nose and his eyebrows all afternoon. It is not obvious that he ought to reply 'Yes', or that his unwillingness to do so is simply a distaste for asserting the obviously true. To say that *S* all the while actually sees whatever is visible before him despite total lack of attention, though not a misuse, is at least somewhat unusual.

V

If one very familiar use of 'S sees D' involves, in addition to D's looking$_n$ somehow to S (i.e. to S's having a visual field that includes D), S's noticing, or attending to, or otherwise acquiring some belief about D, while another use, less usual, is non-epistemic (and may be virtually equivalent merely to D's looking$_n$ somehow to S), the question arises whether one of these uses is more basic than the other. I shall suggest considerations – I do not imagine them conclusive – that may make it not implausible to suppose that the epistemic use is in at least one respect basic or primary. If this were indeed so, non-epistemic seeing might have been shown not to be more basic than epistemic seeing in a sense relevant to the dispute mentioned at the beginning of this paper.

Now it has already been acknowledged that in one respect seeing$_n$ may be more fundamental than seeing$_e$. If 'S sees$_n$ D' is regarded as equivalent to 'D looks$_n$ somehow to S' and if the latter is a necessary condition for the truth of 'S sees$_e$ D', then S's seeing$_n$ D is a necessary (but not a sufficient) condition for S's seeing$_e$ D. It is in this sense, being a necessary but not a sufficient condition, that Dretske for instance explicitly (and surely correctly) claims that his 'primary' seeing-that is more fundamental than his 'secondary' seeing-that ('Unless we could see that c was Q ... in a primary fashion, we could never see that anything was the case in *any* way', p. 157); and (again correctly) that seeing (*his* 'seeing$_n$') is more fundamental than seeing-that ('S sees that b is P in a primary epistemic fashion only if S sees$_n$ b', p. 79). Hence, in this sense of 'fundamental', the one Dretske employs in establishing the primacy of seeing over seeing-that, my seeing$_n$ is more fundamental than my seeing$_e$. But there are other considerations, too, that might reasonably be thought relevant to establishing whether seeing$_n$ has a primacy, in some sense, over seeing$_e$, or vice versa.

One matter, however, should be cleared away first. It does seem that finding out what a creature can see at a given moment (i.e. testing to find out what looks$_n$ somehow to it at t while it is in state F_1) essentially involves finding out what it can notice, pay attention to, respond to or otherwise acquire beliefs about (and I *mean* tests for whether and what it can *see*, not physiological tests of its eyes or other physical organs; see below). The methods of testing what a creature can see are complex to describe but well known, even though we seldom employ them in detail or with great rigour. They are employed in detail by human and animal physiologists and ophthalmologists. Roughly, things are placed or passed before the creature, are moved, their features, colours, illumination, shadows, etc., are varied, and normal experimental safeguards are used to ensure that testers and tested are concerned with the same object. The investigator may have to attract the creature's attention – or try to – to the features he is interested in. Where the test is on humans, he may ask them to talk; elsewhere he watches reactions and responses, often to elaborately devised situations. Appropriate safeguards are required to ensure he is testing *seeing*, not some other sense, which means, roughly, that descriptions or responses elicited are related to properties or apparent properties of light and colour.

If these are the ways in which a creature's visual potentials are explored, we can test and establish beyond doubt a creature's ability to see only so far as we can succeed in directing its attention to objects and their detail. Leaving purely physiological examination aside, our knowledge of its visual capacities is limited by, and depends on, its capacities for attention, noticing and responding to things. (No doubt we might, for some purposes, test a creature's vision, or establish that it is sighted, by *purely* physiological tests; but such tests would not necessarily be conclusive. Indeed they are necessarily derivative from those tests that establish, by a creature's responses, what beliefs it can acquire about its environment.) Presumably, therefore, testing a creature by attempting to direct its attention and elicit responses could fail to reveal its full visual capacities. The investigator who, despite every effort, elicits no 'noticing' response or sign of attention to D may justifiably remain uncertain whether the creature, S, in *any* sense sees D; for if he concludes that S did not and cannot

101

see D, he may conclude wrongly. It is conceivable, first, that a person might actually see$_e$, i.e. notice things and acquire beliefs about them, but not react or respond in any way (ophthalmologists cannot always detect malingering with assurance). Perhaps we may also imagine similar circumstances with other creatures. It seems conceivable that, just as we surely see$_e$ a vast amount of detail, irrelevant to our daily purposes, to which we do not react at all and which we forget almost immediately, other creatures might, even if they do not in fact, notice things which, because of a total lack of practical interest, they never react or respond to at all. Secondly, where the investigator fails completely to attract the subject's *attention* to D, it is correct to say that S *did not* see$_e$ D, but not conclusive that he *could not* have seen$_e$ D; his capacity to see$_e$ may not have been fully exercised or taxed. These are two conceivable cases then where an investigator might fail fully to explore a creature's visual capacities – either because it notices things but does not in any overt way react to them, or because during tests its attention is never successfully attracted to what it could in fact have noticed. The speculation whether cats have colour vision (cf. Armstrong, p. 248) might run along either line. Thus, it seems, what we can discover about a creature's capacity to see$_n$ (or what looks$_n$ somehow to him) depends on what we can get him to notice or otherwise react to, and hence on what he sees$_e$. This gives one kind of priority to seeing$_e$ over seeing$_n$: we do not know for certain that a creature can see in any sense, and cannot conclusively attribute vision to it, unless we find it responding and therefore attending, or seeing$_e$.

But our present concern is not merely with what we manage or fail to find out. Ability to *react* or *respond* does not set logical limits to any concept of seeing, but only to the possibility of testing. It seems not to be an incoherent supposition, for instance, that there might be creatures with as full a *capacity* to see$_e$ as others have (i.e. things do look$_n$ somehow to them, unnoticed) but whose attention is (for perhaps good biological reasons) always *in fact* totally elsewhere. Seeing$_e$, being useless to them, they see$_n$ but never do in fact see$_e$. Doubtless such species, by evolutionary processsess, would not long retain their capacity for vision. But their existence does not seem inconceivable. Thus, in addition to the lesser point already made about testing, which suggested only that it may be a *factual* point, and possibly false, that what we do not get a creature to notice, or attend to, or, hence, to see$_e$, he is incapable of seeing in any sense, there may be something further which, if true, would make seeing$_e$ in a more important way more basic than, or at least as basic as, seeing$_n$. This is that it may be a *logical* point that what a person could not in fact, at a given time by any direction or redirection of attention (all physical factors, e.g. the lighting, his physical state F_1, etc., remaining unchanged), be brought to notice, or attend to, or in short, to see$_e$, he cannot see in any sense. I am suggesting, that is, that if it is in *fact* true that a creature's attention to D could not have been by any means elicited at t while in state F_1, then it must be true not only that he did not see$_e$ and could not have seen$_e$ D at t, but also that he did not see$_n$ D at t. But to suggest thus that, if S sees$_n$ D at t, it is logically required that S should in fact be *capable* at t of seeing$_e$ D and so of acquiring some belief about D, whether or not he did, is to suggest that some broadly mental capacities (to notice, attend and acquire beliefs) are logically tied to any normal or familiar concept of seeing or being able to see. It may therefore be that the elucidation of any concept of seeing and being able to see at a given time must make reference to an ability of the creature that sees to notice or attend at that time to the things that then look somehow to it. Even to say that a creature sees$_n$ something, we do, it may be suggested, make it a condition that he has these mental, or at least more than physical, capacities. I think this position probably characterizes accurately our existing use of 'see$_n$' (and perhaps also of 'having a visual field'). We would surely regard it as conclusively settled that S could in no sense see D (and perhaps that D was not in his visual field), if at a given time we thought he could not, by redirecting his attention, notice, glimpse or spot D. 'He saw D' (and perhaps also 'D looked somehow to him'), 'but by no effort of attention could he in fact have noticed D' is, I suggest, a contradiction.

This point might perhaps be reinforced or emphasized by considering how we might regard cases of complete psychological or hysterical blindness (hysterical blindness is rare, and seems seldom to be total; but such total 'blindness' is surely not inconceivable). Faced with such cases we could not, I suggest, treat them like the real or hypothetical cases previously mentioned where a creature with perfect optical equipment could in fact have attended to the things looking$_n$ to it, but having no interest in them paid no attention to them or was not successfully brought by the investigator to do so. There the investigator failed to explore fully the limits of the creature's vision. But in psychological blindness, while we similarly suppose nothing physiologically amiss to prevent a person seeing, we have reasons to suppose him prevented by psychological obstacles from paying attention to or acquiring any beliefs about the objects then before his eyes; at that time he could not in fact, whatever we did, see$_e$ the objects. Now I suppose we could, if a physiological examination declared his eyes, etc., perfect and the case history pointed to shock or other psychological explanation, choose to maintain that things still looked$_n$ (unnoticed) somehow to him (though to insist thus that he did then have an unnoticed *visual field* would, I think, be simply a decision). But even though we may say that a person who, while temporarily distracted, notices nothing is actually seeing$_n$, I doubt if we would say that the sufferer from psychological blindness is in any sense actually or really *seeing*. It would be natural to say not only that he does not see, but that he *cannot* see. In short, I suspect we restrict all uses of 'see', even 'seeing$_n$', to cases where the person could in fact at the time be got to see$_e$; and it is our notion of *seeing* that this discussion is primarily about (whatever we might *decide* to say about having visual fields, looking$_n$, etc.). If so, this is one reason for thinking that our existing senses of 'seeing' and 'being able to see' involve dual criteria, physical *and* mental capacities, and that no common use of 'able to see', let alone of 'actually seeing', concerns *only* physical considerations. It would explain why being able to see is not simply the negation of being blind, for we do usually employ 'blind' *tout court* in a purely physical or organic sense. We say of the psychologically blind that they are *not* blind, but also, because of the dual criteria, that they cannot see. We coin expressions like 'hysterically blind' and 'functional blindness' precisely to indicate that one condition for seeing is missing but not (it is believed) another. We locate the incapacity elsewhere than in the physical realm. In short, if a creature is incapable in fact of seeing$_e$, i.e. of acquiring certain kinds of beliefs, though we may refer him to a psychiatrist, not a physiologist, and need not declare him physically blind, he is, for all normal purposes for which we use the word 'see', *unable to see*, and to that extent might as well be blind. (None of this denies that in normal eye-testing, where a person's mental capacities are not in question, the doctor or ophthalmologist is interested solely in the patient's physical condition. His report that a patient can see this or that is therefore normally intended only as a report on this condition. But to say of a man that he sees or can see such and such at t is not to attribute to him only a physical capacity, nor are these locutions so used. An ophthalmologist, after inspecting a psychologically blind person, might say, 'He can see perfectly well'; but if he did we should understand this, not as we should understand a report after treatment by a psychiatrist that he is cured and *can now see again*, but as reporting that, though he *cannot* see, he is not organically blind since nothing is *physically* wrong with him.)

It might, I suppose, be argued at this point that the answer to the question whether a capacity to see$_e$ is necessary for seeing$_n$ is not as I claim. Rather, it might be said, there is no obvious answer, the matter being one as yet undecided by practice or rules, and one which we might decide in certain hypothetical circumstances if the necessity arose. I do not think this is so, nor do I rest this claim simply on hypothetical cases of psychological blindness; it seems to me a fact now that we would not say that S could see D at all if he could not, by some effort, notice or be brought to notice D.[8] But if I were wrong and the matter is an undecided one, it would not be the case either that seeing$_n$ does, or that it does not, require the capacity to see$_e$; and the positive claim therefore that seeing$_n$ is, in the sense under discussion, independent of epistemic conditions, being undecided, could not be upheld either.

I shall mention one other possible objection. This is that while animals, insects, etc., can see, as Armstrong says, 'sometimes, we believe, better than we can', it is mistaken or improper to attribute to them beliefs, attention, or perhaps the capacity for any mental states and activities. If valid, this means that though they may, *when* they see, react or respond to their environment as though they had acquired beliefs, it is to over-intellectualize the situation to ascribe to them attention, belief, etc. If the very most that is required for seeing (if indeed even that) is the acquisition of ability to respond or react to what are in fact light stimuli, then belief-acquisition is *not* required. In that case actual seeing, what I have called 'seeing$_e$' throughout and explained in terms of belief-acquisition, has been wrongly described and misnamed. Seeing is a non-epistemic occurrence requiring neither actual belief-acquisition nor even a capacity to acquire beliefs (though, of course, human beings often do acquire beliefs from perception). In short, we attribute vision to many creatures, saying they see D at t, when D (or its real or apparent properties of colour and light) becomes capable of influencing their behaviour at t or after, and even though we cannot attribute attention, noticing, or belief to them.

I think this objection has little if any weight. Certainly theorists on both sides (cf. Dretske and Armstrong) are willing to attribute attention, belief, etc. to animals. In doing so they do not intend to attribute to animals internal debate, deliberation, or the capacity to reflect on themselves or their own states of behaviour. But since it is doubtful whether 'belief' ever carries or has to carry these implications, it is doubtful whether there is anything in the objection. Similarly, the fact that even much adult human behaviour may consist (in Professor Kneale's words)[9] of 'a sequence of unreflective responses to stimuli' does not entail that when human beings are unaware of themselves as acquiring beliefs, attending, etc., they are not in fact doing so. Consequently, unless arguments are given to restrict the notion of belief in this way, it need not be denied that animals acquire beliefs in the unreflective way humans sometimes do.

In any case, the fact is surely that we do employ such concepts as noticing, attending, becoming aware of, learning and knowing with animals, insects, etc., according to and on the basis of their behaviour; and equally clearly we attribute beliefs to them (even if the *word* sounds over-sophisticated) on the same grounds. We say that the dog thought it was about to be fed, that the wasps noticed me and thought I was about to interfere with their nest, that the cat became aware of my presence, and that my movement caught the bird's attention. We make these attributions as far as their behaviour permits, though without necessarily attributing to them self-awareness or deliberative powers. We think that, by using their eyes and ears, animals may pay attention to, learn about and come to know their surroundings, that they can be mistaken, or deceived by appearances. We explore their vision or hearing by finding out what they are and are not capable of noticing, and so on. If they did not exhibit any of this behaviour we would not even say that they can see, hear or smell. Nor am I sure how else we should talk about them if not in terms of attention, beliefs, knowledge, mistakes, etc.

We do employ these concepts with animals then; we attribute seeing and hearing to them only to the extent that we think of them as realizing, noticing, acquiring beliefs and otherwise engaging in activities that involve attention to their surroundings. Perceiving and these other activities seem to stand or fall together. If indeed it is urged that we are mistaken or too anthropocentric in attributing attention or belief to creatures who are unaware of themselves as exercising the one or acquiring the other, we might ask why these are not equally arguments for withholding 'seeing' and 'hearing' from creatures who are unaware of themselves as perceiving.

I sum up so far. I have conceded that in addition to the epistemic use of 'see' there exists also a use of 'see' that is non-epistemic in the sense that such seeing occurs without the occurrence of any belief-acquisition. (This may already be a departure from a wholly epistemic theory. For such a theory would presumably deny any genuine use of 'see' that does not mark an event, in Armstrong's words, of the 'belief-acquiring sort' (p. 224), even while allowing that actual belief-acquisition is sometimes inhibited by 'other, contrary, beliefs'; though perhaps Armstrong's 'idle perceptions' that 'may be conceived of as information that is completely disregarded' (pp. 215, 226, etc.) are cases of seeing$_n$.) But I have suggested that, though a non-epistemic use, 'seeing$_n$', exists, an account of seeing must be ultimately epistemic in the sense that even being able to see$_n$ logically requires, as a necessary condition, the capacity for seeing$_e$, a capacity that is epistemic. I suspect there may also be ways in which seeing$_n$ is secondary to or derivative from seeing$_e$, and consequently other senses in which seeing is basically epistemic; but if the considerations I have adduced have any weight, seeing may already be epistemic in a respect relevant to the initial dispute.

V I

I want now to comment briefly on a number of lesser points. The first concerns that notion of differentiation mentioned earlier in Dretske's additional requirement for seeing something. Differentiation, or perhaps better, differentiability, concerns here the possibility of picking out or isolating something from similar or homogeneous surroundings or background. In discussing this I wish to draw attention to a confusion of two topics concerning vision (and perhaps perception more generally). The central interest traditionally, and rightly, of many who have wanted to discuss vision has been the investigation of what seeing is, or consists in, or how it is to be analysed, or what happens when we see. But discussions frequently take the form, as they do in Dretske, Soltis and others, of inquiring into the truth-conditions of statements like 'He saw Lloyd George (or a deer, or a hill, or a man shaved in Oxford, etc.)' where some particular object seen is specified. Schematically these discussions fasten upon statements of the form 'S saw D' (Dretske) or 'S saw x' (Soltis) where it is apparent that the 'D' or the 'x' are to be replaced, as above, by some name or description of the object seen. So the discussion remains firmly focused on truth-conditions of statements of these kinds. But focusing thus may obscure the nature of what started primarily as a discussion of seeing and was only secondarily about seeing things.

It seems to me that though this inquiry may be interesting enough, it does not represent the central inquiry into the nature of seeing. For if this concerns *seeing*, rather than seeing *a par-*

ticular thing, investigation should be into the truth-conditions of '*S* sees at *t*' rather than of '*S* sees *D* at *t*'. It is likely that the truth-conditions of the latter kind of statement are more stringent, and possible that they might include a differentiation (or differentiability) condition lacking in the truth-conditions of the former. Of course, it might be objected that there is no seeing that is not seeing something or other. But to this, though it is true, two replies may be made. First, there are occasions when seeing occurs (and something or other is therefore seen) without *any particular thing* being seen (all is white mist or blue sky, or, as Dretske says of his example – he calls it a '*limiting case*' (p. 26) – the example of the large smooth wall seen by someone whose nose is touching it, everything that appears to *S* is a part of *D* and '*D* is seen under conditions which do not provide it with an environment'). Secondly, there are occasions (including sometimes occasions when *S does* see some particular thing, D) when we say, and may be willing to say, only that *S sees* (as, when *S* opens and closes his eyes, we might say, 'Now he sees, now he doesn't'). After all, if we ever use 'see' in this way, as we certainly do, there must also be truth-conditions for 'he sees' which make no reference to any particular thing, *D*. So there are reasons for saying that an account might be both acceptable and an answer to the main question about what seeing *itself* is if it set out the truth-conditions, not for seeing *D*, but simply for seeing. But the differentiation condition as introduced by Dretske was of course a requirement for seeing *things* (except in those limiting cases, like seeing the wall, where there is a homogeneous visual field, in which exceptional cases he held the condition to become inoperative). So whatever the case there, I conclude that for *seeing* this condition is never operative, no matter what is seen, since even when it is true that *S* sees some particular thing, *D*, we may limit our statement to 'he sees'. The condition then for *S*'s seeing at *t* will be, for a non-epistemic account of seeing, merely that at *t* something or anything looked$_n$ somehow to *S*; to which is added, for an epistemic account, at least one extra condition, that at *t S* acquired some belief about something or other that then looked$_n$ somehow to him. (Moreover, since we may always say, whenever *S* sees, not merely

109

that S saw but that S saw something (with 'something' used here, as it often is, not to mean some particular thing, D, differentiable from its background, nor to replace some expression like 'a deer' or 'D', etc.), the differentiation condition does not need to be met for someone to see something.) This is why, in analysing seeing, we need not include the differentiation condition.

Nevertheless, even if it is not a central question, or one about the nature of seeing as such, we should also ask whether the differentiation condition must be met (except in the 'limiting cases') for S to see some particular thing, D. I want, however, not to dispute this for the moment but to consider two questions that present themselves if it is so. For this I employ examples that have been used by others. These are the examples of the deer which to the hunter is indistinguishable from the foliage (Soltis, pp. 33, 58 ff.) and of the hill seen (*note* how natural it is to describe the example thus) from the air where the whole landscape below looks uniformly green (Dretske, pp. 25-6). With this kind of example there are two possible positions to adopt, either that differentiability is a truth-condition, or that, though it is not a truth-condition, it is misleading to say, even truly, that 'S saw D' when the condition is not met, and that people therefore normally avoid saying it. Dretske categorically makes it a *truth-condition* of S's seeing the hill that it be differentiated enough from its surroundings for it to have been possible for S, in his position, to pick it out. Soltis, I believe, also makes it a truth-condition, though he repeatedly says, ambiguously, only that we cannot *say* that, e.g. the hunter saw the deer (which leaves open the interpretation that it may be a true, but *misleading*, thing to say. And incidentally, since, as I have already stressed, the question at present under discussion by reference to these examples is whether the differentiation condition is required for it to be possible to say truly 'S saw D', where D is some particular thing, if what I said earlier is right it must be simply a slip for Soltis to say, even with the deer case, that the discrimination requirement is necessary 'for seeing to be said to have occurred', p. 63).

The first question is this. In the hill and deer cases the person, S, may certainly be said truly to see something or other, even if he cannot be said truly to see the hill or the deer. So it is worth asking what he may be said to see. Presumably we must be wary not to say e.g. 'He sees something and the something is a hill/deer' lest it follow from this that he sees the hill/deer. We must therefore provide a schematic formulation that will state what he does see, given that he does not see D and given also that he sees something of which D is or appears as an indistinguishable part, and one large enough to be seen. I think that with a little care this can be done even if in an unwieldy way. For instance, if we say, 'Something among the things, or some part of something, that S saw was a/the D', we have not said that S saw D. If we then add, 'D looked$_n$ somehow to S' (and, for epistemic seeing, also add, 'S acquired some belief about something that was in fact D'), we have said what S saw, and what D's relation to it is, without saying that D is identifiable exactly with whatever we may truly say S saw; D need only have been a part of whatever he may be *said* to have seen, a part nevertheless large enough to look$_n$ somehow or be visible to him.

The second question, still assuming the differentiation condition must be met for S to see D, is what the relationship is between S and D (the hill/deer) if not that of S's seeing D. With these cases of the hill and the deer we feel pulled in two directions. While Dretske certainly, and Soltis probably, regard it as false to say *tout court* that the man looking straight and attentively at the hill or the deer saw a/the hill or a/the deer, it feels equally wrong to deny that he saw the hill or the deer, or that something that he saw *was* the hill or the deer; he was not for the moment blinded, nor were his eyes shut, nor were the objects in question too small for him to see. Indeed, Soltis seems wildly wrong to say that 'we are no better off than the blind man when it comes to the seeing of ... indistinguishable objects [e.g. the deer] with the naked eye' (p. 62). For the hunter may even describe the dappled colours that are the colours or apparent colours of the deer's flank, and, if he is a painter too, (without realizing there is a deer before him) put such coloured patches on his canvas; the airman may similarly describe the homogeneous green that is the colour that the hill is, or looks from above. Hill and deer do look$_n$ somehow to them and they may notice how they look. So if the differentiation condition is a requirement for saying truly that *S* saw the hill/deer, what *is* *S*'s relation to *D*, given that it enables him to describe its colours, paint them, etc.? About certain things I think there is no doubt. First, it is certainly very natural to slip into saying it is seen: e.g. we may say that a deer seen against a similar coloured background may be impossible to distinguish from the foliage and that a hill seen from the air may be impossible to pick out when the whole landscape looks homogeneously green, etc. Equally it seems totally artificial to avoid using 'see' by using some other locution, e.g. that *D* was an object of *S*'s vision. Secondly, it seems natural to say that if someone can do so many things, describe what is in fact the flank of the deer, paint it, etc., he must be able to see the deer, for it is seeing, not something else, that normally makes such doings possible. Indeed, thirdly, so obvious does this seem, that anyone traditionally interested in the nature of seeing would surely have been content to give a satisfactory account of this relationship between *S* and *D* and have supposed himself to have given an account of seeing thereby; it seems good enough to be a paradigm instance of that relationship that perception theorists have worried about. Yet, according to the view under discussion, he would not have given an account of *seeing* something. In the face of these considerations it seems to me very odd to insist that *S* does not see *D*; it is almost as if, although *S* does all that is needed to qualify as seeing *D*, one must not *say* that he sees it. If we do not call this relationship of a person to an object *seeing*, it is hard to know either what would be seeing, or what this relationship is.

I conclude therefore that there is no good reason to deny that the relationship in which *S* is to *D* is anything but *S*'s seeing *D*, or to assert that it is miscalled if called 'seeing'. Consequently, it seems to me correct to say, not only for *S* to see, but also for *S* to see *D*, that no discrimination condition has to be met, rather than to say that such a condition is operative except in certain limiting cases. If this is correct, then to say that *S* sees *D* in these limiting cases is at worst misleading, not false. But I suppose that, so long as it is conceded to me that there is a use of 'seeing *D*' that does not require differentiability, if anyone wished to argue that in addition there is also another that *does* require it, this could be accepted too. We do commonly accept such remarks, in cases like those of the hill or the deer, as 'He looked straight at it but didn't (and couldn't) see it', as well as those like 'He certainly saw it but, understandably, couldn't distinguish it or pick it out from its background'. If we do use 'see' both ways, I do not know why either should be rejected as a misuse.

Next, I want briefly to consider Warnock's remarks in his 1963 *Postscript* on transitive and intransitive uses of 'seeing' and the different sense of 'able to pick out' there introduced. Warnock acknowledges a distinction between 'the ability to see *things*' and the post-operative ability, of a patient who has just acquired vision, to see 'intransitively'. This latter ability is, he thinks, 'a physical capacity' or the exercise of such (on the grounds that 'a blind man may become "able to see" merely in virtue of a physical change, brought about perhaps by surgical operation' (p. 66); I have already mentioned considerations that might make a physical capacity doctrine inadequate). But the ability to 'see things', he thinks, requires more, namely, an ability also 'to pick out or identify' (I ignore the latter), even if this is not actually exercised. Ability to see things is therefore not simply a physical capacity.

Before formulating my dissatisfaction with these remarks I want to dispose of one possible confusion. In my previous discussion the question was whether a person can 'see things' if he is unable to differentiate or 'pick them out'. But there it was a question whether someone saw a particular thing if, no matter how perfect his ability to pick things out, the thing was indistinguishable from its background. For the airman, though in one sense unable to pick out the hill, certainly has, in another sense, an ability to pick out things that the post-surgical patient lacks. He has Warnock's 'ability to pick out', but of necessity cannot exercise it on undifferentiated views; so this ability has nothing to do particularly with the indistinguishability of things from homogeneous backgrounds. In Warnock's use, the normal man who can 'see things' *is capable* of 'picking out', while the man who only 'intransitively sees' is not, even when the visual field is not homogeneous; and the

113

former has this ability despite the fact that, if the background *were* homogeneous, even he would be unable, in the previous sense, to pick out things (or even, if the differentiation condition were necessary, to 'see things').

So far this is only to note one ambiguity of 'seeing things' and to distinguish Warnock's sense of 'ability to pick out' from the one previously discussed. But there are several reasons why the intransitive uses of 'see' need further discussion. Warnock mentions the intransitive use, not simply in a general way, but in connection with those post-surgical cases who are 'able to see', but not 'to see things'. But of course the intransitive use is not limited to those who are unable 'to see things'; as I said earlier, we may say of someone normal, as he opens and closes his eyes, 'now he sees, now he doesn't'. The intransitive use is a familiar way of stating a truth about a *man*, either about his visual capacity or the exercise of it, without committing oneself to his seeing this or that. So presumably the conditions governing 'he sees' will not differ whether we apply it to a normal or a post-operative case. It is simply that, according to Warnock, the normal person has an additional ability, beyond the physical capacity.

I want first to argue that if my earlier comments about the epistemic or more than merely physical character of seeing were correct, even the (intransitive) ability to see, and exercise of it, in the post-operative patient (whether or not he may lack the ability to pick out *things*; see below) is not purely physical; it equally involves a more than merely physical capacity. For the same reasons as were advanced earlier about transitive uses of 'see', intransitive seeing$_e$ will involve *actually* noticing something or acquiring some belief, and intransitive seeing$_n$ will entail the possession of a *capacity* at the time to notice or acquire beliefs. Saying, even of the post-operative case, that at this moment *he sees*, even though this may be used on a particular occasion primarily to draw attention to his changed physical condition (just as, said of the man just cured of psychological blindness, it may be used mainly to announce a return of his psychological capacities), will be true only if he has the more than physical capacity to notice, acquire beliefs, etc. For instance, if the post-operative patient, when he first sees, should unfortunately suffer, almost immediately and perhaps thereby, a shock that renders him psychologically blind, we would not continue to say, I think, *tout court*, that he can see, let alone that he is still seeing, though we now believe his physical capacity perfect. We normally suppose the post-operative case to have certain mental faculties, not to be psychologically blind but to be able to notice this and that, even if only to be baffled and confused by what he notices. So even if the post-operative patient's intransitive seeing does not involve Warnock's more than physical capacity to 'pick-out' and 'see things', the intransitive use of 'see' is no more restricted to a purely 'physical capacity' than are the transitive uses.

The second consideration arises from two facts. The first fact, already mentioned, is that Warnock's 'ability to pick out' has a sense different from that of the deer/hill differentiation. It is not that the post-operative patient has a homogeneous visual field; rather, he is probably unable (partly perhaps because of inability yet to focus *optically* on things) to focus *attention* fixedly enough, to concentrate on this or that, and certainly has not learned yet to isolate item from item and so make sense of the varied panorama before him. This is certainly a primarily psychological incapacity which time and experience may or may not rectify. It is an inability to pick out one *thing* (in a strong sense) from another because of inability to determine spatial relationships, to distinguish the edges of things from their shadows or from colour variations on their surfaces, and so on. The second fact is that, though we may use an intransitive *locution*, no actual seeing (whether seeing$_e$ or seeing$_n$) is logically intransitive. Whenever someone sees, something is seen, whatever the seer makes or fails to make of it.

Taking these two points together, the question is whether, and how far, there is truth in Warnock's suggestion that ability to see 'intransitively' does not require ability to pick out 'things', whereas ability to 'see things' does. I think that what happens is that a third sense of 'ability to pick out' comes to light and a further ambiguity of 'seeing things'. I will set aside one possible complexity that concerns the point at which, after surgery, a man can be said to see. If the operation had secured only a limited capacity, like the residual vision in pre-surgical cataract sufferers, for merely telling light from dark or vaguely that something, say a light, is moving about, there would be a question whether the patient (who in some sense certainly cannot see *things* or learn to, being still under an extreme physical handicap) can be said to see. I will ignore this complexity by supposing the surgery completely successful as far as the patient's optical capacity is concerned. Can we now say that (intransitively) he can see, indeed, can see perfectly? No doubt we can if our purpose is to stress the physiological facts alone (though I have questioned already whether even this ability to see is solely a physical capacity). Let us call this 'intransitive seeing$_p$', to stress the physical aspect (and we must remember that, depending on the success of the operation, seeing$_p$ will be capable of degrees). But can we say, with Warnock, that this ability to see intransitively involves neither ability to see things nor ability to pick out? I defer this for a moment to consider another point. I think it certain that there is *another intransitive* use of 'see' that we do *not* employ in the immediate post-operative period until the patient *can* pick out and differentiate things, at least pretty well. Until then we do not say, *tout court*, that he can see, and certainly not that he can see perfectly. To say, with this relatively full-blooded *but still intransitive* use, that he can see requires him to have learned to pick out things in a good deal of detail (and so to be able to 'see things'). In these contexts, medical and psychological writers talk indeed of *learning* to see. So there is, it seems, an intransitive use, call it 'seeing$_t$', in which a man cannot see until he *can* pick out (and see) *things*. Consequently there will also be part-way stages when, though his physical cure is complete (he can see$_p$ perfectly), since he cannot yet always separate objects from movements of shadows, etc., he can as yet, even intransitively, see$_t$ only moderately well.

But to return now to the question whether seeing$_p$ either involves, or as Warnock holds, does not involve an ability to pick out and see things. If the foregoing is correct, though one intransitive use (see$_t$) does involve such an ability, another (see$_p$) does not. But I said a third sense of 'picking out' and 'seeing things' comes to light. In the immediately post-operative situation, after the perfect operation, as soon as S sees$_p$ intransitively, there *is* a sense in which S must already be capable of picking out what are, in a weak sense, 'things', and therefore must be able, in a weak sense, to 'see things'. For instance, he must in fact have some ability, whether yet exercised or not, when there is much movement of doctors and nurses, to notice, and to that extent pick out, what are *in fact* things. He must be capable of noticing that many changes of some sort, movements, variations in his visual field, are going on, these being in fact the doctors, nurses, their shadows, etc., moving about. So though we might sometimes refuse to *say* that he can see things (see$_t$) on the ground that ability to pick out *objects* from mere *shadows*, etc., is necessary for the truth of such a statement, it is evident that some capacity, in another sense, to *pick out* or notice or distinguish differences in the colour, lighting and movement of what are in fact things, and so, in some sense, an ability to 'see things', is as necessary to intransitive uses of 'see' as to transitive uses. Anyone who lacked in some degree the capacity, in this weaker sense, to pick out things – a surely more than physical capacity since it involves attention, concentration, memory, etc. – could not only not intransitively see$_t$; he could not intransitively see$_p$ perfectly either; and anyone who lacked it entirely could not intransitively see$_p$ at all.

VII

I tried earlier to explore the plausibility of an epistemic account of seeing in which seeing$_e$ was fundamental in the sense that no creature can see in any way unless *able* to see$_e$. Thus, the actual seeing by reference to which other kinds are analysed involves actual acquisition of beliefs. Consequently anyone who exercises this capacity to see, even for the first time, must acquire some belief. Without strongly committing myself to this view, I suggested that a resolution of the epistemic/non-epistemic dispute in favour of the former might be at least not impossible. If therefore a basically non-epistemic account, making no reference at all to belief, is ultimately correct, positive arguments to establish it are still needed.

I return now to my suggestion at the beginning (Section II), that even if an epistemic account is tenable, epistemic theorists may have been incautious in developing their accounts. For instance, the beliefs acquired, even if they might have to be of some particular kind, need not be of the kind apparently envisaged, for example, by Armstrong. (I say 'apparently' because his account seems to me unclear or ambiguous. Taken according to the interpretation to which his words and examples most readily lend themselves, his account of the beliefs in the acquisition of which seeing consists seems to me unacceptable.) Since all primary instances of perceivings, on the epistemic view, are instances of belief-acquisition, it is worth trying to indicate how these beliefs must be described for this view to have any hope of success (provided it can survive objections from other sources) and what the pitfalls are that it must avoid. I emphasize again that I am considering only the *belief* component of such theories. Any full epistemic account of seeing (or perception) would have to face and resolve a further very considerable range of questions, e.g. about how to exclude *non-perceptual* ways of acquiring these same beliefs. These would include questions about the causal ancestry of the beliefs, the part played in that ancestry by the thing seen, the requirements (logical or factual) of light, proximity of the thing, sense organs, etc.; questions, in fact, about what would rule out not only the acquisition of similar beliefs from informants, but also (if these ought to be ruled out too) beliefs analogous in content that might conceivably be acquired, in imaginary and non-routine ways, about remote objects, or in darkness, or by creatures without any (apparent) light-sensitive organs. I do not comment on these questions since, as I have said, I am not attempting to formulate an epistemic account. My aim now is only to comment on the necessary condition that some belief or other must be acquired and on some ways in which the belief can and cannot be specified.

It is, of course, obvious that even if *some* belief must be acquired, the range and variety of beliefs acquired by normal beings might be enormous. They might, but need not, be beliefs (true or false) about what the features, properties or status of the thing seen *are*; equally they might be about what the thing's features, etc., merely seem to be. They might be beliefs that only a sophisticated and experienced creature could have; and they might be about non-visual properties of things, e.g. that the pavement is wet (not just shiny), or that someone is becoming embarrassed (not just going red in the face), etc. No doubt, too, the beliefs might have to be restricted or related in some way to a certain content, so as to be beliefs about, or derived from, visual phenomena or the visible aspects of things: light, shade, colour, etc. (the proper objects of vision), not sounds or tastes. But this I cannot discuss. All I wish to do, given that some belief is necessary, is investigate the minimum belief that S might acquire which would suffice for S to have seen D. If an epistemic account is to stand any chance of success, creatures who can certainly see must not be endowed with more sophisticated concepts than they might in fact have; yet they must be credited with whatever concepts are necessary for seeing. Thus, even if much else needs to be specified to complete an epistemic account, some statement about the belief-component should be possible specifying the minimum belief-acquisition that, given other conditions, would yield a sufficient condition of seeing. This minimum might be not only the minimum that such an account must require, but also the maximum that an epistemic account of seeing can require if the theory is to be applicable to infants, etc.

I mentioned earlier that one consideration that leads to a belief-acquisition account of perceiving, and which leads Armstrong to his version of that account, is the supposition that any alternative must admit, in addition to physical and public things, other *substantival* 'non-physical sensory items' (p. 217), 'experiences', 'sense-data', etc. Such items, if thought of as the 'basis for our perceptual judgments' lead supposedly to the difficulties of Phenomenalism or Representative Perception, or else remain 'mere phenomenological accompaniments of our perceptual judgments'. Another consideration perhaps, even if 'experience' is interpreted as a verb, not substantivally, is the difficulty of describing seeing and other species of perceptual experiencing or awareness, because they are, unhappily, as Moore said long ago, 'diaphanous'; it helps if something as non-diaphanous as acquiring a belief can take their place. But perhaps most important, as providing a positive incentive to a belief-analysis, rather than merely reasons for avoiding other accounts, is the argument expressed by Armstrong thus: 'It is clear that the biological function of perception is to give the organism information about the current state of its own body and its physical environment, information that will assist the organism in the conduct of life. This is a most important clue to the *nature* of perception. It leads us to the view that perception is nothing but the acquiring of true or false beliefs concerning the current state of the organism's body and environment' (p. 209). The first two sentences of this quotation are doubtless true. They point to the conceptual truth about the 'nature' of perception that it is (at least centrally) necessarily concerned with states of our physical environment (and perhaps of our bodies). We do not consider occurrences of hallucination, when we do not become aware of items in the physical world, as cases of perception, or not as primary cases. The primary concept of perceiving has not only what Armstrong calls 'existence-grammar' (p. 215) but also physical-existence grammar. This central use of 'perceiving' certainly embraces the five senses, though I do not wish to legislate at all about its boundaries, e.g. with after-images. But though it is the 'nature' of perception to be concerned with elements of the physical world, and even if perception of these physical things may consist in the acquisition of beliefs, this does not establish the position Armstrong is led to in his third sentence, that whoever perceives is necessarily acquiring beliefs (true or false) concerning things, events, or states of the physical world. For this conclusion is ambiguous and, as he seems to interpret it, in the absence of discussion to the contrary, false. If a creature had, and continued to have, *no* conception of a physical world, he might still see what are in fact physical objects, and whatever beliefs he might then acquire in seeing would be, in one sense, beliefs *in fact* about physical objects; but he could not, in another and stronger sense, be described as acquiring beliefs about the physical world. The conceptual truth about perception establishes that 'perceptual experience' is the acquiring of beliefs about the environment in the *former* sense, but it does not establish that it is in the latter sense; yet this, with some questionable exceptions, is the sense Armstrong's discussion seems to give it. It is probably a fact and, if not, certainly conceivable that creatures who *already* perceive have to learn that the capacity they have is a capacity to perceive. They may have to learn that they possess faculties which by their nature are in fact (in a convenient Lockean expression) 'conversant about' their physical environment, in order to realize that they can employ these faculties to acquire beliefs about that physical environment. Even if it is a necessary truth that a creature who perceives is acquiring beliefs that are *de facto* about its physical environment, it is a contingent fact, if a fact at all, that it will acquire any beliefs about the physical world in a sense that requires it to have some conception of a physical world and environment. Unless this ambiguity is avoided, a belief theory is liable, as I think it does with Armstrong, to endow creatures with concepts that they do not, perhaps cannot, or at least conceivably need not, possess, as a necessary condition of their being able to see.

The principle that has to be followed is that no creature can have a belief without having the concepts requisite for that belief. As Armstrong himself says, 'If perception is the acquiring of beliefs or information then clearly it must involve the possession of concepts. For to believe that *A* is *B* entails possessing the concepts of *A* and *B*' (p. 210). To this I would add what Armstrong omits to mention, that it also entails possessing the concept 'is' of predication or property possession. The other principle I shall follow is that, in being 'committed to the view that there can be concepts that involve no linguistic ability', we are normally justified in attributing a certain belief to *S* only if *S* is capable of responses appropriate to having the concepts and belief in question. We can attribute to a dog the belief that its master is about to take it out, but not that he is about to take it to the park rather than to the common if the dog's behaviour, as the master picks up the lead, never exhibits any appropriate differences that would permit the alternative concepts to apply. The main question, about the minimum beliefs attributable to those who see, must be approached by considering creatures who lack experience, like human infants and the animal young (as well as imaginary examples), whom we certainly speak of as seeing, no matter what other experience or senses they may have or lack. Whatever cannot occur in their cases cannot be necessary for seeing. So given, for example, that infants see, what belief-acquisitions can or must we attribute to them?

First, I have agreed that in every case of perception S must acquire a belief about something (D) which, whether A knows it or not, is *in fact* some feature in its environment. But from here there are ways we obviously cannot go on. For instance, I shall argue in a moment that though it is necessary that D must look$_n$ somehow to S, it is in no way necessary that S should notice or acquire the belief that D looks$_n$ somehow. Moreover, it is at least open for discussion whether or not we might sometimes have to attribute possession of the concept 'looks$_n$', or at least 'seems$_n$', to a creature before it has acquired, or its behaviour indicates, any possession of the concept 'is'. In any case there is nothing that requires us to attribute to a creature who sees any belief that something *is* P (where P is any property), or with it the concept of property possession (by which I intend, very broadly, the notion of something's being such and such). But if Armstrong's 'beliefs concerning the environment' is taken in the stronger sense that I attributed to him, there is at least one concept, more crucial than any of the above, that, it would seem, any creature who sees at all must possess. Yet it is a concept that many creatures, at some stage of early infancy, may surely lack, even though they can as surely see. I shall call it the concept of *status*. By a status concept I mean such concepts as those of physical bodies or public bodies, or of things external to, or independent of, one's experiencing. (The status concepts that contrast with these are those of the non-physical, non-public, non-external, etc. I imply nothing about whether a creature could acquire either the former concepts or the latter without acquiring contrasting pairs. Nor do I imply anything about the possibility of acquiring the concept of property possession before or without some status concept.) I need not claim (what is doubtless true) that some infant creatures *do* see before acquiring (as revealed by their behaviour) any members of these pairs of concepts, or that they acquire them slowly and partly as a result of perceiving. Whatever the *facts* about the young of sighted species, it is certainly conceivable that a creature might need to acquire, and partly indeed by using its vision, the concepts of external status and of itself as being a physical organism in a physical world; and if this is even conceivable, the notion of a creature seeing without these concepts is conceivable. (It is needless, therefore, to comment on what are facts beyond much doubt, that human infants acquire these concepts through visual and tactual exploration, that other small animals do so also but often much more rapidly, and that some creatures perhaps, in certain minimal respects, may behave instinctively as if they had these status concepts.)

If, then, it is either a fact or possible that some creatures who see possess no status concepts, seeing cannot be the acquiring of beliefs that employ such concepts, and any belief-analysis of seeing that requires this is ruled out. And surely there seems no absurdity in suggesting that when a creature actually sees *D* (a physical object), it may have not only no conception of something being (in any of a variety of senses) private, or inner, or non-physical (either as pains, or after-images, or hallucinations are), since there might *be* no such phenomena, but also, more importantly, no conception of something's being outer, physical, external to its body, independent of its perception, or at a distance in space (just as later it might have as yet no conception of distinctions between such items in the physical world as objects and shadows). To establish that *S* sees *D* we need not establish from its behaviour that it has any such concepts or beliefs. All we need do is simply establish that it reacts in some suitable way, reveals that its attention is taken by *D* or by changes or apparent changes in *D* (e.g. by following *D* with its eyes, just as, if it hears, it may start or cry out when there are loud noises). Given such successful tests, *we* may be justified in saying it sees *D*. But our question is what belief we can attribute to *it*.

It seems that the minimal belief we could attribute to it would be the belief (however brief or momentary) that *something* existed or happened (and that we might attribute this belief even though we cannot attribute to it the belief that something *is* somehow or *looks* somehow. The responses and behaviour of the creature towards *D* (which I am assuming

123

are such as to satisfy *us* that they are *visual*, responses to light, dark, colour, etc., not to sounds) need never exhibit any indication of its having any conception of physical status, distance, space-occupancy, etc. It need not, for example, having as yet not explored or co-ordinated sight, touch and its own movements, exhibit any tendency to reach out for things that it follows with its eyes. At some point when it begins to do this, it is beginning to behave in ways that allow us to attribute to it concepts of physical or external status. But in so far as the infant's behaviour towards things (which it is in fact seeing) is consistent equally with its taking or not taking them to be external, nothing in its behaviour favouring the former rather than the latter, we cannot justify attributing to it an external status concept. The principle governing what it makes sense to say of the infant is the principle employed in all other cases where we attribute beliefs, discrimination and experience generally to others. Positively, the responses are (even if minimal) as if the creature believes or realizes that something exists or is happening; negatively, nothing in its behaviour shows it has the concept of 'a thing before it'. But if the most we can attribute to it is the belief that 'something ...', we are using 'something' as a concept *inclusive* of distinctions that *we* can make and that it may later learn to make, without implying anything as to its being able to make them. This 'something' is inclusive in a way analogous to the way 'looking$_n$' was earlier; it covers disjunctions between which we, but not the infant, can distinguish. Using 'something' here partly parallels the way we say of the dog only that it thinks that *someone* is at the door, when its behaviour never differentiates between its master's tread and that of others. This need not prevent our saying, in an over-specifying way of the dog who *can* distinguish its master's tread, that it thinks its legal owner is at the door; but we take this only as indicating that it thinks Smith, who is its legal owner, is there, not that it has the concept of a legal owner. So, when we can sensibly attribute to the infant a belief indefinite enough to cover various specific beliefs but cannot commit ourselves to the infant's having the concepts required for those more specific beliefs, *the referent* of the term 'something' may be a physical thing, but the belief we attribute does not involve the concept of something with external status, even though we may *say*, e.g., that it noticed that a flash of lightning occurred. So also later, as the infant develops, we may somewhat similarly attribute to it a belief that something moved, where this time 'something' can be interpreted as specifically covering (and perhaps limited to) various public phenomena, but not implying that it can make as yet any distinction between things and, say, shadows.

I introduced the non-status-indicating concept 'something' to suggest that a creature who actually sees might manage merely with this and without a particularized physical-status concept. I did this (*a*) to refute one overparticularized kind of belief theory, and (*b*) to specify a concept that, if any belief-analysis is to be tenable, it would sometimes be necessary and sometimes sufficient to incorporate in the beliefs acquired in seeing. Similarly, there would seem to be what I might call the minimal 'verbal' concepts that, on a belief-acquisition theory, it would suffice for a creature to have if it is to see. A creature could have seen *D* if he acquired the belief that something (interpreted as above, and where the something was in fact *D*) *existed* or *happened*, where these are similarly non-committal uses of these verbs. That is, the creature's belief need not involve concepts of *physical* or *public* existence or occurrence (or, if one insists on interpreting 'exists' and 'happens' in that way, the creature need have only such inclusive concepts as would correspond to our 'existed-or-seemed-to', etc.) Provided that the something it believes to have occurred can, by reference to the creature's responses, be identified by us with *D* (the flash, moving object, or whatever, that is seen) this seems to be both the most we have to attribute by way of belief and also perhaps the bare minimum that a belief-acquisition account can operate with. The same considerations apply to 'is there' if the belief we attribute to the infant is that 'there is something there' or that 'something is there'.

I suppose it worth noting again at this juncture that while I have interpreted Armstrong's epistemic theory as one that attributes to creatures who actually see certain concepts, including the status concept of an external object, which they conceivably could lack, there is also that other use of 'see', discussed already in Section VI as 'seeing$_t$', according to which a creature has to *learn* to see and cannot see until it has. This use, in which the post-surgical patient whose sight has been restored perfectly cannot yet see because he cannot yet pick out *things*, and in which infants may not yet have learned to see, but the more basic capacity, that is under discussion by external status concept. But it is presumably not this capacity to see, but the more basic capacity that is under discussion by philosophers of perception, including Armstrong. Creatures can learn to see only if they already have, and only by exercising, that other capacity to see which infants have, which the blind may acquire by the help of surgery, and which cannot be acquired by any learning.

I have interpreted Armstrong's epistemic theory by taking his 'acquiring of beliefs about the physical world' (p. 208) in the stronger sense. In attacking it I have stressed what he himself admits, that if S's seeing necessarily involves S's acquiring a belief, S must possess the concepts involved in that belief; and this, on the stronger interpretation, would mean that S must have the status concept of a physical thing or of a physical environment. It might be thought that I am trading on a mere infelicity in Armstrong's statements and that, though these are verbally compatible with the stronger interpretation, he really intends the weaker view I indicated. But if so, not only does he seem not to note the ambiguity explicitly or attempt to remove it, but the main tenor of his account suggests the stronger view. It seems incontestable that his views on illusions, hallucinations and mistakes all bear out this interpretation; nor otherwise would he need his increasingly complex and epicyclic stratagems to explain 'perception without belief' either as the acquisition of belief-*tendencies* inhibited by prior beliefs, or else as *derivative* from belief-involving cases (pp. 223-4). These are not only implausible (as requiring infants to possess prior beliefs that inhibit even their earliest perceivings from being beliefs *about their environment*); they smack of *ad hoc* theory-saving to avoid accepting supposedly exhaustive alternatives. The fear is that if 'perceptual experience' is to be '*distinct* from the acquiring of *beliefs about the environment*' (p. 217, my italics), then it will become 'some relationship that the mind

126

has to non-physical sensory items' which will 'stand between our mind and physical reality' (p. 226), such items being either grounds on which we base 'beliefs about the physical world' or mere 'phenomenological accompaniments of our perceptual judgments'. To avoid this unwelcome situation, with its 'postulation of sensory items', he adopts the other extreme, denying that our perceptions are distinct from our acquirings of beliefs about the environment and hence also that they can be 'the basis for our perceptual judgments' (p. 226). He does consider, but only momentarily, the possibility of finding a third way by admitting 'the notion of perceptual experience as something quite distinct from the acquiring of beliefs about the environment' without admitting the non-physical sensory items, but adds ' I have been unable to see how this can be done' (p. 217). The weaker and non-specific belief-view I have suggested provides precisely this sort of way out. Perceptual experience involves no non-sensory items; it is the acquiring of beliefs that are, in the weak sense, *in fact* about our environment. However, these beliefs are not themselves, but become the basis of, beliefs about the environment in the strong sense. This view, even were it supported only by hypothetical cases, which it is not, is not only more plausibly true; it disposes of the need for his stratagems. A creature perceiving will *always* be acquiring a belief of some sort, not an inhibited tendency to believe, and perception will still be, necessarily, a possible source of information about the physical environment. But the creature perceiving need not realize that the capacity he has is of this perceptual sort, or himself acquire any beliefs about the environment in the strong sense. Consequently this weaker view also needs none of Armstrong's complications to deal with 'perception without beliefs', since no case of actually seeing, will occur without some *actual* belief-acquisition. But since these need not be beliefs *about the physical world* in the strong sense, inhibition by prior beliefs is not necessarily required either.

If it is arguable at all that Armstrong does *not* intend the stronger view that requires status concepts, this must rest on the brief remarks he makes about 'immediate and mediate perception' (pp. 233 ff.); but here I find it impossible to draw out any clear enough interpretation to put the matter beyond doubt. He connects the notion of 'immediate perception' with that of 'sense-impressions' and restricts these to the acquirings of beliefs 'involving the sensory properties of the sense in question' (p. 236) (but still speaks of them as 'beliefs about the current state of our body and environment' p. 237). But despite the importance for a belief-theory of clarifying the beliefs and concepts that the perceiver may have, or that might be attributable to him, Armstrong does nothing to spell out these beliefs or concepts but leaves the matter with the remark that 'the particular content that sense-impressions have is a matter of psychological theory' (p. 237).

In any case, putting aside questions about the interpretation of Armstrong, if I am right, the minimum belief possible, but also sufficient, for seeing would be that something in an inclusive sense 'existed' or 'happened' (where the something was in fact D and D in fact looked$_n$ somehow to S). Though adult creatures normally acquire more complex beliefs, that something is P, or merely looks P, or looks$_n$ P, or seems$_n$ P, etc., it is not necessary to attribute to S such beliefs as these. As I hinted earlier, an infant need not be credited with the concept 'is' of property possession (and possibly could not have it without some physical status concept). Nor, I may add, need it have (nor perhaps could it have) any predicate concepts, like green, smooth, bright, shiny, bent or spherical (in connection with each of which the use of 'is' may need to be separately learned). Nor again, even if at some stage an infant might be credited (on the basis of its behaviour) with some such inclusive concepts as 'looks$_n$', (as contrasted with 'sounds$_n$', 'feels$_n$', etc.), does he require this, or even 'seems$_n$', any more than he requires 'is'. No doubt the behaviour of animals and infants begins at some point to indicate (and so justifies us in attributing to them) a realization that they are employing one sense, not another, just as it indicates at some point that they believe things to be external or physical occurrences. But just as, for it to be a case of vision, the belief need not be (when what was seen was a flash) that something *bright* occurred, so it need not be that something *looked$_n$* somehow. The situation can occur in adult as well as in infant life, when for instance we know that something (*in fact* a slight change in the lighting) disturbed our concentration, that we cannot say whether it was a change of lighting, a slight sound, or what. Its being a matter of *looks*, i.e. of *vision* (and hence of light, colour, etc.), need not be incorporated in the belief of the perceiver.

On any account of perception there is need to work out in detail the relations between the less and the more sophisticated beliefs we acquire by, say, vision. But I have not been concerned with this here. However, if the beliefs of a creature who sees may sometimes be, and have to be, as rudimentary as I have suggested, any theory that analyses seeing in terms of acquiring more complex and sophisticated beliefs, *or inhibited inclinations to such sophisticated beliefs*, must be in error (and an error of a similar kind to that of those sense-datum theorists who suppose that those who perceive may initially acquire the beliefs, say, that something *is bent*, or *is elliptical*, beliefs that are subsequently to be inhibited or corrected by later experience). Consequently I have doubts not only about such views as Armstrong's but also about views that Vesey has expressed.[10] He says that 'All seeing is seeing as' (p. 73) and explains this by saying that 'if a person sees something at all it must look like something to him' or 'looks to him to have some quality' (p. 83). This I take to involve a confusion of uses of 'looks'. It is true if it involves only 'looks$_n$'; but it is false, I think, if it involves that opinion-indicating use of 'looks' that I mentioned briefly earlier (p. 90 above) which concerns S's having an opinion about how it looks$_n$ to him. If my arguments are correct, S may see D without having any belief about *how D looks* to him, or even any realization that it does *look* somehow to him at all. S need not have either the concept 'looks', or any predicate concepts, or the concept of 'being like something', or that of 'having a quality', or of the 'is' of predication. But Vesey's view that 'what an object looks like to a person is what he would judge that object to be if he had no reason to judge otherwise' (p. 83) does seem to imply what I have questioned: if not that S believes *that* something looks somehow to him, at least that S has an opinion about *how* it looks to him (say, P, or like a D), and that, without

129

reasons to judge otherwise, he would judge it to *be P*, or a *D*.

VIII

I have not attempted to develop a belief-acquisition account of seeing. But I have argued that, if such an account is to be tenable, it must apply to all creatures who see, including infants. No doubt many concepts are acquired and used in seeing; but many are not required. This must eliminate the kind of view I attributed to Armstrong. Since, however, on any epistemic account some concepts are required, the minimum that will suffice would seem to be the rudimentary 'something', and 'existing' or 'happening', in the senses explained. The infant who, for the first time, hears a noise or sees a flash and jumps or cries must be held at least to think that something happened. The holder of this theory must also presumably hold that the first occasion on which an infant sees may be the occasion of acquiring some such concepts. He may think of babies in some way as the following. Prior to the first occasions on which they see$_e$, they may, though physically capable of seeing, be, like the psychologically blind, incapable of attention; consequently they do not yet see. Even when the ability to attend develops, it may be for a while not yet exercised; so they perhaps see$_n$, but still do not see$_e$. Even on their earliest occasions of noticing anything (seeing$_e$), though they of necessity acquire some beliefs and perhaps the rudimentary beliefs already mentioned, *we* may have no grounds for attributing such perceivings to them. Their moments of attention may be so short lived, their physical ability to focus so poor, their memories so short that there may be nothing in their behaviour or responses to suggest to us, as there is in those momentary but attention-catching circumstances when they jump or cry, that they have seen or heard anything. But, like the child who sees the flash and does jump, they are acquiring at least such momentary beliefs as that something exists or has happened. Something like this, whatever the other features of his account, would seem to be Armstrong's view: 'At a certain instant the perception occurs.... But this state disappears so rapidly – the impression fades so fast – that we

130

may well be reluctant to describe it as a state of belief. The state is gone before there is any possibility of a manifestation of belief.... This very description ... shows that there is here no threat to our analysis.... There is no reason why we should deny this possibility' (p. 233).

By this time a belief-acquisition account may seem so whittled away that some might regard it as wholly trivialized and be tempted to regard accepting or rejecting it as a matter of insignificant choice and decision. But any epistemic account, whatever else it requires, must commit itself to the possibility of some such minimal beliefs and concepts as those I have indicated. If this is too odd or far-fetched, all versions of an epistemic account must collapse for this same reason. There would therefore be no need to examine other possible difficulties, or develop other features, of such accounts; we could switch to developing some form of non-epistemic account at once. But though no existing epistemic account to date has faced or dealt adequately with questions about the content of beliefs acquired (or, for that matter, with those other difficult problems that do not concern the belief component), it is not obvious to me that these questions about belief present any insuperable problem. There may perhaps be other conclusive difficulties; but an obstinate holder of a belief-acquisition theory might not only cite in his favour those considerations that earlier I suggested as favouring such a theory; he might also reasonably claim that, even if ultimately untenable, this kind of account has not yet been shown to be so, and that a satisfactory alternative has yet to be provided.

Notes

1. G. J. WARNOCK, 'Seeing'. Page references are to the reprint with Postscript, 1963 in Perceiving, Sensing, and Knowing, ed. Robert J. Swartz (New York, 1965).

2. FRED I. DRETSKE, Seeing and Knowing (London, 1969).

3. D. M. ARMSTRONG, A Materialist Theory of the Mind (London, 1968).

4. It is important not to suppose that the beliefs one acquires in

seeing, if seeing is to be analysed as the acquiring of beliefs, can be easily characterized, or that I have committed myself to any species of beliefs. They have to be 'about' the thing seen in a non-obvious way on which I say something in Section VII. They must be characterized in a way that ties them to light and colour, and so to *seeing*; and they must be acquired in some sense directly or non-inferentially. But my intention in this paper is not to develop an epistemic account of perceiving, only to show that one may be possible or necessary.

5. J. F. SOLTIS, *Seeing, Knowing and Believing* (London, 1966).

6. A. M. QUINTON, 'The Problem of Perception'. Page references to reprint in Robert J. Swartz (ed.), op. cit.

7. IDA MANN and ANTOINETTE PIRIE, *The Science of Seeing* (Harmondsworth, 1946).

8. I do think, however, that, while the question whether such a person could then *see D* in any existing sense of 'see' is not a matter that awaits explicit decision (all existing uses of 'see' requiring a capacity to see$_e$), there may be no clear answer, without a decision, to the question whether a thing's looking$_n$ somehow to *S*, or *S*'s having an unnoticed visual field, has the same requirement. If this does await decision, then *S*'s seeing$_n$ *D* and *D*'s looking$_n$ somehow to *S* will not be virtually equivalent as I have so far assumed for the sake of argument.

9. See above, p. 66.

10. G. N. A. VESEY, 'Seeing and Seeing As'. Page reference to reprint in Robert J. Swartz (ed.), op. cit.

II

GODFREY VESEY

Professor Sibley (*a*) distinguishes two different kinds, sorts, notions, senses or uses of seeing, (*b*) distinguishes two opposed 'accounts' of seeing, according to which one, or the other, of the two different kinds, etc., of seeing is basic, fundamental, or that by reference to which the other is to be analysed, (*c*) considers arguments for these opposed accounts, and (*d*) tentatively comes down on the side of one of the accounts. The two different kinds, etc., of seeing are what he calls 'non-epistemic' seeing and 'epistemic' seeing. Non-epistemic seeing is described by reference to the writings of Dretske and Warnock, and to what Sibley calls 'non-epistemic looking'. Epistemic seeing is described, in part, by reference to the writings of Armstrong, and to the concept of belief. The account on the side of which Sibley tentatively comes down is that according to which epistemic seeing is basic.

His treatment of these matters is a long and involved one. Rather than try to say a little about all the points he makes, I'm going to raise just one issue.

The issue concerns senses of the word 'looks'.

It is my contention that Sibley has a blind spot for that sense of the word 'looks' that is crucial for an understanding of the connection between seeing and believing.

The senses of 'looks' Sibley recognizes are:

   (i) what he calls '$looks_n$' ('non-epistemic looking')
and
   (ii) what may be called the 'tentative (or firm) opinion-indicating' sense of 'looks'.

The recipe Sibley gives for '$looks_n$' implies that the '$look_n$' of something is determined by such things as the laws of perspective. The name of the other sense of 'looks' is self-explanatory.

The sense for which Sibley has a blind spot is distinct from both the perspective-determined sense ('looks$_n$') and the tentative-opinion-indicating sense.

An example may serve to illustrate the three senses.

Below is the Müller-Lyer figure.

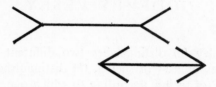

The two horizontal lines are in fact the same length.

Suppose Sibley were asked 'Do the horizontal lines look unequal in length?' If he knew that they are in fact equal in length, his reply would have to be either:

(i) 'If one were attempting a *trompe-l'œil* depiction of them on a flat canvas one would have to draw lines of equal length. So in the "looks$_n$" sense of "looks" they look equal in length.'

or

(ii) 'Since I know that they are equal in length I am not of the opinion, even the tentative opinion, that they are unequal. So, in the opinion-indicating sense of "looks" they do not look unequal.'

Against Sibley, I maintain that there is a third sense of 'looks' in which the lines look unequal in length even to someone of whom it is true (i) that the lines look$_n$ equal to him, and (ii) that he is not of the opinion that they are unequal.

This third sense is not analysable in terms of the two senses Sibley recognizes. When I say that the Müller-Lyer lines look unequal I do not mean, for instance, that I am of the opinion that they look$_n$ unequal.

I shall call this third sense of 'looks' the 'epistemic' look ('look$_e$'). One thing that can be said about it is that what an object looks$_e$ like to somebody is what, on looking at it, that person *would* believe it to be, *if* he had no reason to think otherwise. The Müller-Lyer lines look$_e$ unequal in length to me: if I hadn't good reason (having measured them) to believe them to be equal, I would, on looking at them, believe them to be unequal.

(The situation is complicated by Sibley deciding to make 'to S', in 'D looks$_n$ ø to S' function not only as a 'physical situation indicator' but also as an indicator of the condition of S's 'eyes or other physiological apparatus'. I am far from sure how this is to be understood. If the Müller-Lyer illusion is to be explained by reference to our 'eyes or other physiological apparatus', does it follow that the lines in the Müller-Lyer figure look$_n$ unequal in length to us? Suppose there is a physiological explanation of the 'reversal' which takes place as we look at the duck-rabbit. Does it follow that it looks$_n$ at one moment like a duck, at the next like a rabbit? Since I don't know what Sibley would say, I won't pursue this line.)

It is hard to believe that Sibley is quite unaware of this third sense of 'looks' ('looks$_e$'). In fact, I don't think he is quite unaware of it. It creeps in by the back door, so to speak. Writing on the opinion-indicating sense of 'looks', he remarks that 'she looks exhausted' may be a way of 'saying that one thinks (or is inclined to think), from the way she looks, that she *is* exhausted'. In the Müller-Lyer case, this would be: ' "The lines look unequal" may be a way of saying that one thinks (or is inclined to think), from the way they look, that they are unequal.' *From the way they look.* This cannot be the opinion-indicating sense of 'looks' again, for it is a reference to what serves to justify one's opinion. And it is not the perspective-determined sense of 'looks', for in that sense of 'looks' they do not look unequal.

Sibley seems, here, to be relying on the third sense of 'looks'. But he does not admit it.

Let us consider the consequences of not admitting it for our understanding of the connection between seeing and believing. If Sibley intends 'looking$_n$' to be understood in terms of the recipe he gives – that is, in the perspective-determined sense – then while the look$_n$ of something to somebody can be said to be true *to* the object of which it is a look, it cannot be said to be true *of* the object. It can be said to be true *to* the object in the sense that, given particulars about the observer's physical situation *vis-à-vis* the object, one can correlate features of the 'look$_n$' of the object with features of the object, by means of the laws of perspective. Indeed, one can go further. Given particulars about the lens of the eye, one can correlate features of the retinal image with features of the object. And I suppose that given particulars of the retina, and of the optic nerves, one can correlate features of the nervous impulse with features of the object. Finally, given particulars of the brain, one can, I suppose, correlate features of the state of excitation of the brain with features of the object. The perceiver is not, of course, aware of the retinal image, or of the nervous impulse, or of the state of excitation of the brain. But there has traditionally been supposed to be something mental, a 'sense-impression', corresponding to the state of excitation of the brain, of which he *is* aware. Perceiving has traditionally been thought to consist of two things: (*a*) sensing this sense-impression, and (*b*) making a judgement that is, somehow, based on it. The trouble with this piece of philosophizing is that no one has succeeded in giving an account of how the judgement is based on the sense-impression, which does not, in the end, involve the denial that we can know anything about the external (*sic*) world by using our eyes.

Unlike the look$_n$ of something to somebody, the look$_e$ of something to somebody *can* be said to be true or false *of* the world. (The look$_e$ of the Müller-Lyer lines is false of the world.) There is no gap, between what *cannot* be said to be true or false of, and what *can* be said to be true or false of, the world, to be bridged. It is because of this that the epistemic sense of 'looks' is crucial for an understanding of the connection between seeing and believing.

At the beginning I said that Sibley tentatively comes down on the side of an account according to which epistemic seeing is basic. Can I agree with him on this, at least?

There is a sense of 'see' that corresponds to 'looks$_e$'. It is sometimes referred to as the 'see as' sense of 'see'. To say that D looks$_e$ ø to me is to say that I see D as ø. In this sense of 'seeing', it is a conceptual truth that seeing is a reason for believing. It would cease to be so if its analysis did not involve believing (that is, if it were *not* the case that what an object looks$_e$ like to somebody is what, on looking at it, that person would believe it to be, if he had no reason to believe otherwise). But, equally, it would cease to be so if seeing were defined in terms of the opinion-indicating sense of 'looks'. My being of the opinion that D is $\emptyset$ is not a reason for my believing that D is $\emptyset$. There simply has to be a 'looking', and a 'seeing', which has a foot in both camps, but not both feet in either, if seeing is to be a reason for believing.

The Temporal Ordering of Perceptions and Reactions

I

BRIAN O'SHAUGHNESSY

I INTRODUCTION

Frequently we react more or less immediately upon perceiving something. Yet beneath this general characterization there exists a wide multiplicity of phenomena, ranging from acts based on 'snap' decisions, through high-speed responses to sudden perceptions, and terminating in the case of sheer shock. It is my contention that an *internal episode* characteristically intervenes between perception and inception of act; that we achieve increasing immediacy of response with some cost to the status either of the act as act or of perception as perception or of both; and that there is no such thing as a temporally instantaneous, novel and active reaction to perception. Therefore any supposed causal relation between act and perception cannot be described as temporally immediate. And to the extent that temporal immediacy is in the mind a necessary condition of *immediate causality*, it looks as if *such a causal bond* cannot here obtain.

The cases that we are most prone to put forward as clear examples of an immediate mental causality between act and perception, high-speed or automatic response, prove in fact to fall between the two stools of internal and external determination of response. We try to have the best of both worlds, to combine the novelty and immediacy of shock with the activity of action, but stumble instead upon a kind of temporal Indeterminacy Principle. For we have the illusion that automatic cases provide the spectacle of two clear-cut phenomena, perception and action, temporally smack up against one another; whereas the truth is that, to the extent that an internal episode

is absent and the activity of action retained, to that extent
the whole concept of temporal ordering drops out of the picture.
An indeterminacy obtains which cannot be remedied, for it
is an indeterminacy that merely attests to the inapplicability
of a concept. Thus, we make the mistake of confusing the
primitive with the causal – a common enough mistake
nowadays! High-speed response, a primordial contact of human
reality with the world, prior to and not engineered through
thought, is a primitive, albeit essential, example of perceptual
response. This paper has not the space to consider the phenomenon of shock, but examines the other two central cases:
snap decision and high-speed response. It is primarily concerned with questions of *timing in the mind*, and in particular
with the specific question of the temporal relation of reactive
act to perception; and since time is the fundamental category
for mental events, due weight must be attached to such an
enterprise. We shall begin by considering the temporal placing
of events in general in some detail.

II THE TEMPORAL ORDERING OF EVENTS

(A) *Comparing the placing and ordering of objects with that
of events*

Where is an object? What is its location? Which is its place?
It is no more where its centre of gravity is than where any
other point is that it is at, nor is it merely at all points on or
within its boundaries, though it is at all such points. The object
is *in* the space bounded by its boundaries: it lies in that space.
Then when is one object ahead of another? It is nearer to any
selected external point, and therefore ahead in that direction,
if the gap between it and the point is less than that between
that point and the other object. And the gap is the space
between point and object, and given in measure by the smallest
line in the set of lines from that point to all points on the
object's surface: a one-dimensional measure of a separation
in three-dimensional space! Therefore, a car is nearer to any
point beyond its surface, it is ahead in any direction leading
away from itself, so far as its occupants are concerned. But
because these concepts are relative to choice of point and

direction, in no absolute sense is any object ahead of another.

It is different with time. The sinking of Venice, which we will suppose to have happened between 1800 and 2800 and to have lasted a thousand years, is neither earlier nor later than, neither after nor before the XXXth Biennale. It did not take place at the same time, but all the while the latter was happening the former was happening. Thus, we cannot temporally order events if the temporal boundaries of one include those of the other. So how do we order events if they overlap? And how, if one or both are temporally more or less extensionless?

But first: what is an extensionless event? While change in traffic lights might take 10^{-2} seconds and involve continuous transition from orange to green, this event takes in our perceptual experience exactly *no time*. There is neither qualitative nor temporal differentiation in the experience: we are aware of neither beginning, middle, nor end of the change in colour, and say neither 'I saw the beginning of the change' nor 'I saw the beginning to be of the following character'; and therefore this event occurs in our experience at a mere point in time. Then because we cannot, from the start and *in toto*, drive a wedge between the general experiences of mankind of temporal extension and the temporal extension therein experienced, our concepts must enable us to draw a distinction within the class of events analogous to that between point and line. This distinction, which cannot be reduced away, is constantly employed in the ensuing discussion.

(B) *The ordering of events*

(1) *If both event e′ and e″ are extensionless*

Then either they are simultaneous or an interval exists between them, in which case one is after the other: e.g. the traffic lights went green after going orange.

(2) *If e′ is extensionless and e″ extended*

(*a*) If the non-autonomous event that is the beginning of e″ is later than e′, then e″ comes after e′: because the car began to skid after the lights went green, the car skidded after the lights went green.

(*b*) If e′ is later than the ending of e″, then e′ comes after e″: e.g. if the lights went green after the car came out of the skid, they went green after the skid.

(c) If e' is simultaneous with the beginning of e'', then neither comes after the other: e.g. if the car went into a skid as the lights changed, the change did not precede or follow the skid. Now because the latter change was at t', while the skid took place between t' and t'', these events were no more simultaneous than is the location of England that of Land's End; and yet one happened while the other began to happen. What we notice in this case is that, although sectors of e'' are later than e', e'' is not later than e'.

(d) If e' coincides with the ending of e'', then the position stated in (c) is reversed.

(e) If the moment of e' falls within the temporal boundaries of e'', then e' is neither before nor after e'', and neither does it happen at the same time as e''; for e'' does not happen *at* that t_x but was instead happen*ing* at that moment, and thus the space of time that they occupy is not identical. For as the material object is timelessly passing through any interior point at which it is, so the event spacelessly extends through every interior instant in which it is happening: the 'at' of the object resembling the 'ing' of the event. For example, the moment at which the lights changed was a moment at which the car was skidding.

(3) *If e' and e'' are both extended continuous events*

(a) If the end of e' is earlier than the beginning of e'', then e'' comes after e': e.g. the sinking of Venice came after the building of the Parthenon.

(b) If the bounds of e' fall within those of e'', then e' is neither earlier nor later than e'', yet e' happened while e'' was happening, even if it did not happen at the same time as e'': e.g. while Venice was sinking I paid it a visit.

(c) If they overlap as one object overlaps another, then one is later than the other: e.g. Bradman's Test career, 1928-48, was later than that of Hobbs, 1909-30. By contrast, if a man smoked a cigar after drinking a liqueur, the end of the drink was no later than the beginning of the smoke, and because it does not follow that he smoked after finishing drinking, we distinguish 'He smoked after drinking' from 'He smoked after finishing drinking'. It seems, therefore, that we cannot say that

Bradman's career came after that of Hobbs. And if a man had a liqueur and then had a smoke, as opposed to starting drinking and then starting smoking, the smoke was after the drink, and again this does not imply that the beginning of the drink was after the end of the smoke. Thus, 'He smoked after drinking' does a different job from 'He started drinking and then started smoking', from 'He started smoking after finishing drinking' and from 'His smoking was later than his drinking'. Each performs a distinct task, even though they are all consistent with one another. It therefore seems that with time, as with space, we are on the one hand interested in an ordering that is along merely parallel lines, like the ordering of runners in parallel tracks, whereby one event is said to be later than another if it measures up to the criteria of the present paragraph, 3(c). On the other hand, we have the ordering that is that of succession, which as it were takes place along a single straight line that can accommodate no more than one event at a time, an ordering that is applicable to those cases that meet the criteria of 3(a) and/or those following in 3(d).

(d) If the time of the non-autonomous event, the ending of e', is the same time as that of the beginning of e'', so that the events have a point in time in common and so touch temporally, then e'' comes later than e', e'' comes after e', e' happened and then e'': e.g. we say 'The stone rose and then fell', 'The stone fell after rising' and 'Falling was later than rising', but not 'The beginning of falling came after, or later than, the end of rising', or 'The stone stopped rising and then began falling'. Further, and this confirms our earlier suggestions, we say neither 'The stone stopped rising and then fell', nor 'The stone rose and then began falling'. Now this form of succession, in which a moment is shared, is possible only in the case of extended events, and is akin to that of carriages in a train.

The above analyses indicate *what we assert* when we say that one event stands to another in one of the following temporal relations: simultaneity, being later than, coming after; and we should here note that the distinction between coming later than and coming after only has substance in the case of two extended events. Now according as the two events that are said to stand in such temporal relations are extended or exten-

143

sionless, the criterial implications of such claims vary in the ways above indicated.

III SIMULTANEITY AND CONSCIOUSNESS

The relations sketched above obtain in physical nature, and accordingly the above criterial implications obtain there also. The theory and technology of physics enable us to import new standards of temporal measurement and order, so that an event can be timed to 10^{-6} seconds and situated that much later than another. Conflict about temporal placing between a lay public and scientists is no more real than conflict between a draughtsman who says 'This line is perfectly straight' and a scientist who says 'It deviates by 10^{-3} mm from perfect straightness'.

Simultaneity is an essential temporal dimension in human life. Through perception we are aware of many phenomena, some simultaneous with one another, some not; for example, at t' the traffic lights changed, at t' the car began to move, at t' man first contacted the moon. Because the last of these events is visible only 1·3 seconds after it occurred, we distinguish 'happened simultaneously' from 'were simultaneously perceptible from here'; but since most events in perceptual experience are local, the distinction has merely exceptional application – and I shall sweep the problem of sound under the carpet. In perception we are aware, at any moment, of phenomena that are simultaneous, and *as* simultaneous, whether unified in a sense field or not. And even if we are short on phenomena, sight at any moment displays the state of a surrounding region at that moment.

It would be impossible to speak of *the state of a region* unless we could in addition speak of *its state at a particular time*. If we could not, chaos would spread into the supposed description of the state of the region, since time holds it together. For it is a description that might at first appear to consist in an enumeration of the state of the (totality of) continuous spatially ordered fragments of that region, each fragment, let us say, either at some random time out of all possible times or else at a point in some ordered continuity of changing

144

times; but because this in turn involves the description of the state of a fragmentary subregion of the region, at some one of all possible times, and because we rejected this possibility, nothing could pass under the heading, 'description of the state of a region'. Therefore the concept of *such* a state is a concept of pure chaos: it is nothing. Therefore, if sight can inform us of the state of a region, it can inform us of the state at a certain time.

True, the visual field frequently divides in two so far as temporality is concerned, one half informing us of simultaneous local phenomena, the other of temporally scattered stellar events; but if our relation to all perceptible phenomena was like that to stellar phenomena, variously and haphazardly strung along a set of temporal threads, perceptual information, and with it consciousness, would not exist. A man set drifting in outer space would have the simultaneities of his previous history, together with that of present thought and sensory and bodily experience; but even the latter would cease to be if there were no such thing as simultaneous awareness of the simultaneous *as* simultaneous. To repeat: the concept of information would dissolve, and with it those of perception and consciousness. One could imagine a sense field in which such divisions as that of earth from stars were repeatedly duplicated, but not one in which they were in general duplicated limitlessly. The very concept of perception rests upon the simultaneous presentation of the simultaneous *as* simultaneous; even though the latter 'as' functions cognitively rather than perceptually.

But might not the visual field divide in two, into relatively near equidistant stars and further equidistant nebulae; and might we not *know* this? And would not the simultaneous presentation of those simultaneous items as simultaneous with one another, in each of these halves of the field, fail to come as simultaneous with their presentation to consciousness?

To be sure, and this also runs counter to the general character of perception, whose primary function is to inform us of the truth of the here and now state of the world: 'now' uniting here and over-there as one here, 'here' doing the same! Thus, in general perception requires the simultaneous presentation of the simultaneous as simultaneous, and as simultaneous

145

with that presentation. At the same moment x, we experience an a and b which are happening at the same moment y, and we experience a and b as happening together at some time z, and x and y and z are one. It is this way essentially with touch, essentially so also with sight as perception of the local environment, and therefore this way typically with sight. The change of this hammer head at this point to red at t', and of that hammer handle at that point to red at t', both perceived at t' and in suitably abutting regions in the visual field, will be integrated as perception of the change of a hammer to red at t'. *Therefore* the perception of anything qualitatively and spatially differentiable depends upon the perception of the simultaneous as simultaneous. The perception of such complex phenomena involves the integration of non-autonomous part-phenomena into a single sense field, and in addition their integration with consciousness in the single instant, t', for each must be seen to happen together at the t' of the phenomenon.

In sight the information provided by the sense comes in spatially-temporally-conceptually differentiated form; for the perceived objects extend in space and are perceptually presented as spatially interrelated, the sense field is occupied at any point by something of a certain kind, and it is liable to change its content at any point at any time. It is of the nature of sight that the spatially and conceptually differentiated information, such as this half of a chair going yellow and that half of a chair going yellow, come as simultaneous if they are simultaneously perceived. Without a temporal framework in which to fit such information, that information would not be; for the framework is not like that provided by a filing system, which does no more than harbour already gained information. The order is, in short, constitutive of the ordered. The very concept of consciousness rests upon the co-presenting of experiences, perceptual and other. Temporal ordering holds consciousness and self together.

If the diversity of space generates the simultaneous co-presentation of simultaneities as simultaneous, and as simultaneous with their presentation, the diversity of time generates the successive presentation of successive events as successive. In perception we experience events as temporally ordered, and this order is characteristically that of the events themselves, which in turn is determined by perceptual consensus. The situation in which the lights change after a star explodes, though the star is seen to explode seven years after the change of lights, is far from typical and returns us to an ultimate. Therefore we cannot conclude from the findings of science that our general impressions of the simultaneity of extensionless events are probably incorrect, mere makeshift classifications of almost certain non-simultaneities. We admit there is a sliding scale of accuracy, comparable to the difference between 'The road runs in a perfect straight line for ten miles' and the draughtsman's 'This line is perfectly straight', and leave the matter at that.

IV THE VARIOUS ROLES OF 'AND'

(A) *The 'and' of enumeration*

If I mention a set of events, whether causally related or not, in a linguistic enterprise, I may divide mention of each event off from its neighbours by the use of 'and'. Then, depending on the nature of that enterprise, I can in saying something of form, '*x* and *y* and *z*', be variously understood. I shall not call these different senses of 'and', but because in each case 'and' can be understood as involving the suppression of a different phrase or sentence, sometimes to be understood as 'and the next event of that kind to happen was' and sometimes as 'and therefore', I will speak of them as ' "ands" of different kinds'. Just as we prepared the way for a discussion of the ordering of psychological events by considering that of events in general, so we now wish to prepare the ground for a consideration of the role of the separator-term 'and' in the psychological report by a general discussion of the roles open to this word.

First, there is the 'and' of enumeration. But it is never sheer enumeration, unless we mean a random selection of events. Even then, what is mentioned is events, as opposed to objects; for there are no random enumerations of 'just anything', since if 'just anything' is *not anything* then there can be no such enumerations. We cannot enumerate *nothing*! Then if I speak of the 'and' of enumeration, I do not mean that we enumerate under no heading. Rather, that some enumerations are lists and no more, whereas other lists are subordinate to further enterprises: say the enterprise of describing a single complex object or event. Think of describing an irregular sinuous line: how each descriptive addendum helps to constitute a more complex totality that will in turn become a structured structurally placed part of the next totality, each addendum mentioned under a unifying heading that makes of it the latest element of a developing totality: a continual unifying principle of narration. Or of the various meaningful stages reached by a lengthy melody. And as an example of the enumerative 'and', in which we simply list, irrespective of interrelation, items whose only posited interrelation is the external one of falling under a specific heading, we might instance the listing of objects or events of a certain kind within a region of space or space-time: for example, objects in a drawer or noteworthy events at a party. Then need these lists be *disordered*? A list of books on a shelf might be a spatially ordered list, and yet a mere list; and the same holds concerning time.

(B) *The 'and' of temporal narration*

(1) *The narrative 'and' and its application to consciousness.*

By contrast, there is the 'and' of temporal narration, the link in the 'story line' so to speak, which in part entails the placing in temporal succession of events of a certain kind. The 'and' of sheer enumeration may here be employed without contravening the narrative project; e.g. in enumerating the multiple objects of a momentary perception which is mentioned in the narrative in a single complex sentence ('he saw *a* and *b* and *c*'); or else in enumerating, in conjoined sentences jointly preceded by 'at time *t*', the multiple events that constituted a certain stage of a complex event (at the same time he saw *a* and felt *b* and heard *c*').

What is the narrative 'and'? The narrative employing the narrative 'and' takes as its subject-matter the development of *a continuity*, whether simple or complex; and clearly this is of great relevance to our overall enterprise, since it is the general form of inner life, which is a continuous on-going flux.

The character of this 'and' shows in the following. Compare (1) 'He entered the room and the contents of his pockets moved and his gastric juices stirred', (2) 'He entered the room and felt the gold in his pocket and experienced a desire for a drink', (3) 'He entered the room and walked to the bar and ordered a drink'. Each may enumerate a temporally ordered set of events of a certain kind in a region of space-time. But whereas (1) is probably no more than that, (2) and (3) probably occur as part of a story; and generally do so if intended as such. If so, then in (2) and (3) the temporally ordered list will be subordinated to describing the development of a continuity.

We are inclined to say that in (2) that continuity is one of *awareness*, in (3) of *occupations*, and that it is in either case the continuity of *a single process*; but this position has difficulties. While his relation to his actions is not that of observer, he is aware both of what he is doing *and* the contents of sense experience. Further, his actions do not take place *in vacuo,* for agents mostly employ their senses in acting, and can be described only if that description mentions his selective awareness of his environment. Moreover, his future actions can later be described only if the narrative has already mentioned prior and seemingly irrelevant perceptions – which in turn entails the need to interrupt a narrative of occupations by instancing such intersecting perceptual events – or else turn back the clock in the narrative and include those events by devices other than the narrative 'and'. It is for these reasons that we cannot separate off narratives of action and awareness.

The extremely important narrative of *the individual consciousness* is one that mentions *action* and *perception* and *thought*. Some perceptions occur within perceptual activities like looking, while perceptions like hearing a clap of thunder generally do not. Actions characteristically relate to an environment which is thus perceptually and actively revealed. And while some thoughts are reached through an active enterprise of thinking, some either stem from perceptions or else simply emerge from the depths of the mind. We shall see, in VII(D) and VII(E), that the natural interrelation of the processes within consciousness does not necessarily make of them a single complex active process. For example, a looking that

149

is absolutely subordinate to a motor or mental activity is yet distinct from them; and nothing could override this crucial distinction within being. Then let me say, here and now, that this form of unity is the most in the way of overall unity within the mind that we could ever hope for. Thus, even though consciousness probably necessitates that one have some occupation at any time, and the occupation characteristically magnetizes to itself other activities, nothing prevents us from engaging in a number of simultaneous, distinct and unrelated occupations. In any event, the characteristic unity of mental contents shows, not just at the instant, but through time; and this has repercussions on the form of the narrative. Because the world is not *a one* – for the unifying heading 'item in the world' cannot make these items into merely differentiated elements of the one thing – the most unified consciousness cannot but contain diversities of being; for in relating to the world we relate to that which of necessity cannot intrinsically mirror the unity of the unifying project. Therefore, even subordinated perception is an enterprise that of necessity lies open to the extraneous, and for this reason alone it could not be actually assimilated by the dominant enterprise. Unity is therefore *most nearly achieved* in moments of rapt and intent activity, but *never actually achieved*. Now the principle of the narrative of the individual consciousness is that the narrative neglects those elements of consciousness that are both diverse and extraneous. While it mentions the temporally ordered contents of consciousness, it is not the description of a single complex activity or process. All that we mention falls under a heading, but the heading is not such as to unify into the one flow. The stream of consciousness, while a unity, is not one.

(2) *The integration of subcontinuities and discontinuities into the narrative of the continuity.*

Yet that a complex conjunctive sentence expresses more than an enumeration turns on matters quite other than the presence or absence of a connective consciousness. For one might describe the continuous spatial history of a piece of flotsam: how it drifted, then rose and sank, how it rose again, then slowly revolved; and this, too, is some kind of story. The wood might at one and the same time advance, waver, rise and veer, and these processes might be non-autonomous sub-processes that are integral to its continuing movement through space.

But what of angular movement? This is not movement *through* space, since the revolving object does not leave its space behind, so much as movement *in* space, and here it is the parts of the object that of necessity put space behind themselves; and yet one mentions it now under the heading of movement. Angular movement does not disappear into linear movement, whereas veering and rising are axis-relative differential elements in a description of linear motion. Even so, because angular and linear motion are not unrelated – for any combination of linear and angular motion entails a certain linear path for each point of the object – their subsumption under movement is genuine. Neither embraces the other, each could exist without the other, yet they are integrated when occurring together, and, as we shall see in VII(B), they might be either autonomous or non-autonomous. Thus while these two processes are more than differential elements of a description, they do not fall apart as necessarily unrelated processes. Therefore in a narrative the mention of wavering and veering and angular motion will be conjoined by the 'and' of enumeration if they are simultaneous, and by that of narration if successive. Thus, a narrative of a single process can include mention of non-autonomous subprocesses; and a narrative of related but perhaps distinct processes may include both autonomous processes like angular motion or non-autonomous processes like a non-distinct rising that accompanies advance.

Then is it not open to us to add to the history of the flotsam an item of the following kind: 'at t' it was touched by a fish'? It depends on the theme of the narrative, and thus on how we would continue. It might be integrated into a history of its dynamic progress, as cause and occasion of a shift of path, in which case we omit change in appearance, and the enterprise is not purely spatial, but spatial and perspicuously so; for if it were purely spatial, we might mention contact with a fish as a mere pointer to the time, as opposed to an explanation, of a development in motion. But it might instead find mention as part of a wider narrative under the heading 'Experiences of a piece of wood'; and along with this we would mention changes of colour and shifts in its path. The latter is somewhat akin to the enterprise of describing the continuity of consciousness: spatial shift being akin to action, contact with fish to perception, and the consequent shift akin to a reaction to perception. The former enterprises resemble the attempt to describe continuity of action independently of perception – an impossible project, if only because man relates to the environment differently than does wood. We see here how a narrative can incorporate not merely subprocesses, autonomous or not, but discontinuous events, and this is possible because they either time or explain, or both, present or later developments in the process.

(3) *Stages in the development of the narrative schema: the integration of event intersection and simultaneities.*

The narrative of a particular continuity can be very simple, and can take a temporally translucent form. But it is not always simple; indeed it turns out to be a potentially rather complicated schema. Thus, did the man, in (3) above, order a drink before, or after or simultaneously with reaching the bar? It was after, though the narrative declines to say whether he paused before ordering; and this it must if it is to be exhaustive. Then compare (3) with (4). 'He entered the room and walked towards the bar and heard someone call out'. (4) displays the devices we employ to cope with the problem posed by event intersection, to indicate that one event happened before another was complete; and having said what it has to say, it might yet advance the narrative by employing the 'and' of narration in adding 'and when he reached the bar', so indicating that the narrative advances through all three events: beginning to walk, hearing, reaching. Faced with this complication, a dual one since the discontinuous event is integrated into a continuous narrative and also cuts across a continuous event, the narrative can retain complete precision in temporal communication.

The further complication of simultaneity can be introduced into the narrative by means of 'as', 'during' or 'while', without contradicting its narrative character. Thus, we can say (5) 'He entered the room and walked towards the bar and heard someone call out and reached the bar and as he did so he caught sight of Smith and he ordered a drink'. Entering and walking and ordering stand in the relation of succession, though the narrative fails to indicate whether they touch temporally at one point; though it would, if exhaustive. For if these are the only stages of a single continuous process, they must touch; but in (5) this can be so only if consciousness is continuous and the subject continuously occupied by his activities; and a necessary condition of this latter is that he be occupied in a single activity that unifies all three. But the narratives (2) to (5) leave us in the dark on whether or not this obtains. In (4), hearing is after beginning to walk – and we require such differential expressions as 'beginning' to make these very orderings – reaching is after hearing and simultaneous with catching sight of, and ordering may or may not be after reaching and catching sight of.

What temporal relations occur then in 'He reached the bar and as he did so he caught sight of Smith and he ordered a drink'? It is possible to contrast this narrative with '... and as he did so – he caught sight of Smith and ordered a drink'. Does this last suggest that the sight of Smith can be 'stomached' only with a drink to wash it down? It depends how it is intended: whether as explanatory, or else as a pure chance simultaneity. If the latter, 'x and as he did so, y and z' will be used interchangeably with 'x and as he did so, z and y'. If explanatory, such interchangeability will not be possible, but neither will the temporal relation be specified: for it is understood neither as 'and then', i.e. as the next point passed through by the on-going narrative, nor as a non-chance simultaneity expressible as 'and so and at the same time', nor as indicative of a suspicion that perhaps seeing *just* preceded ordering. It simply fails to say.

Again, what temporal relations obtain in 'He reached the bar and as he did so he caught sight of Smith and he ordered a drink'? First, it is clear that reaching and seeing are simultaneous, and that ordering is after the approaching that ends in reaching. Then if the 'and' in '... Smith and he ...' furthers the narrative, ordering is after both reaching and seeing. However, if the narrative is to be read as '... and as he did he

153

caught sight of Smith and ordered a drink', the question then arises as to whether this is an explanatory sequence. If it is, then the above time relation is unspecified; but if it is a mere assertion of simultaneity, this will show in our readiness to interchange narrative order and introduce 'and as he did' after 'Smith'. In these somewhat complicated ways the temporal relations may be made clear. Now if the subject is continuously occupied in an activity, and if (5) details all the stages of the activity, the relation must be one of simultaneity: the moment of reaching will be that of beginning to order, and seeing must occur at the point of touching of two temporally extended successive events. In that case the sight of Smith did not initiate a new action, for the developing activity flowed up to and moved continuously past this point.

We have considered the complexity introduced into narrative by the sheer enumeration, either of objects in the instant, or else of events in the instant; and in such cases the narrative neither advances nor stops, but as it were marks time. In addition to this, there are the complexities of event intersection across a part of a process, itself integrated into narration, and of simultaneity, of which the same may be said. In all these cases the time direction was preserved, in a narrative enterprise that was dedicated to the description of what is essentially advancing through time. This holds even when the process involves non-autonomous subprocesses. But what of those processes, like certain examples of rising or of angular motion, where it is distinct and yet integrated? What of the narrative of a complex public event like a party? Because the *dramatis personae* at a party thread their individual paths through time, this narrative cannot proceed uniformly in a straight line; for example, if the narrative is to get under way, it is not really open to us, by means of the merely enumerative 'and', to strand all the invitees to a party at the door, like so many Zenonian arrows waiting to be advanced through time. Now the disparate incidents that will condition the description of later stages of the process cannot be subsumed under the heading of the developing process in a single individual ('the life and soul'), as with intersection and simultaneity, for the incidents occur in autonomous units or subgroups whose developing history is relevant to those later descriptions. It is therefore necessary for us to trace through time some of the history of these individuals or temporary subgroups, return to the beginning and do the same for others, and so on. Nevertheless, the 'and' is still that of narrative and temporal order, first because we trace these items only a certain distance ahead, and then only in bits, in order to advance the narrative through time on a broad front; secondly, because retracing is achieved by the use of additional expressions like 'at nine o'clock', 'earlier' or 'meanwhile', and therefore the 'and' is supplemented by what is not suppressed, as in 'and earlier in the night at nine o'clock Jones had arrived' – the tense of 'had arrived' indicating that the narrative has already reached a certain stage and can adopt a temporal standpoint on the earlier stages of the complex event being described.

Other narrative schemata exist also. For example, that employed in *Rashomon*, where our interest in a set of incidents is by design subordinated to concern with the attitudes to those incidents of the participants: in particular, with their capacity for the acknowledgement of guilt. Each participant purportedly narrates the same events, and by the end at least some of the distortions stand at least partially unmasked, and are at once jettisoned and yet retained as implicit internal narrative, while what remains is harder or softer fact reached through individual consciousnesses. Throughout the succession of individual narratives a further narrative occurred, at right angles as it were, passing from the distortions of subjectivity in the direction of fact, perhaps never to reach its goal. And while this narrative is that of the incidents, it is nonetheless by means of the schema subordinated to an internal narrative in depth. This is the function of the schema: a gloomy and pessimistic device, since its interest in subjectivity is almost wholly critical.

(C) *There is no 'and' reserved for recording a merely suspected temporal order.*

In physical nature we encounter the following temporal situations, and the following kinds of reports.

Suppose I witness two events I know to be causally unrelated. Here all the relations sketched in Section II(B) can obtain.

155

(α) I see these traffic lights change (1) as, (2) after those lights change.

(β) I see them change as I hear you (1) begin speaking, (2) speaking, (3) end speaking.

(γ) I see them change (1) before you start, (2) after you have finished speaking.

(δ) I heard thunder (1) at the same time as I heard, (2) all the time I heard, (3) before, (4) after, (5) during the singing of a song.

(ε) The match on court 2, 4-6 p.m., took place later in the afternoon than the match on neighbouring court 1, 2-4.15 p.m.

Sometimes I cannot decide which is the correct description. For example, I may be unable to decide whether the lights changed as you began speaking, or just before. Then I might say, 'It may perhaps be that the lights changed a moment before you began speaking', as a perceptual report. Now if I take two simultaneous events, and irrespective of whether I consider them to stand to one another in explanatory relation, it is possible for me to mention them in an orderless list that is a mere list of events of a certain kind; in which case I use 'x and y' interchangeably with 'y and x', employing the 'and' of mere enumeration. Alternatively, I might mention them in a spatially ordered list that is no more than a list, in which case I cannot use these expressions interchangeably; or else they are in this very same list spatially simultaneous, in which case they would be linked by the 'and' of sheer enumeration and the expressions would be used interchangeably. But suppose, on the other hand, that I experience the two events, x and y, successively. Then here too I might place them either in a sheer list of enumeration, or else in one whose principle of order is spatial, or in one whose principle of order is temporal; and in the last two cases I cannot use 'x and y' interchangeably with 'y and x'. Now from the fact that temporal succession generates one sentence order if the enterprise is mere temporal listing, while simultaneity does not, it does not follow that there is a special use of 'x and y' whose purpose is to indicate the direction of *my suspicion* in those cases where I am unsure of the temporal order. There is no use of 'The lights changed

156

and you began speaking', as opposed to 'You began speaking and the lights changed', which is specially tailor-made to preserve the suspected, but as yet unselected, time order. At such times we employ 'It seemed perhaps to me ...', and the like.

This fact is important, as we shall see later, in considering cases of high-speed automatic response, for there we encounter a preferred order that we are inclined to interpret in the way I have indicated. That is, we tend to misread the 'and' in these cases as helping to indicate a suspected temporal order, whereas in fact it is the 'and' of explanation or causality.

(D) *The 'and' of causality*

Suppose I witness events I know to be causally related. Again, all the above temporal relations obtain. Yet my report, dividing mention of each event by means of 'and', need not mention these temporal relations.

(α1) Metal touches metal and the lights go green.

(α2) There was a flash of lightning and a crack of thunder.

(β1) The contact effected in pressing the button effected completion of the circuit and the lift rose.

(β3) The rock fell and hit the ground.

(δ3 & β1) There was a sudden tremendous downpour and the river rose.

(ϵ) It rained all night and the river rose.

What kind of 'and' do we encounter in these reports? It is the 'and' of causality, which is to say merely that the listing enterprise is subordinate to an enterprise of stating a cause and its effect; and this enterprise is to be contrasted with one of stating, without regard to order, pairs of events that stand in causal relation. As a way of exhibiting the 'and' of causality, let us consider the ordering of events in a sentence reporting a causal sequence, in a case where these events are not temporally separable in our perceptual experience. I do not perceive the breaking of a bottle to be later than its contacting the floor, nor a difference in time between the contacting of two pieces of electrified metal and the commencement of movement in an ammeter needle. Therefore I cannot offer a perceptual report that is a temporally ordered narration of these phenomena, though I could in special circumstances simply

157

list them, whether under the heading of events at a certain time in a spatio-temporal region or else as events in that region which stand in causal relation to one another. Nevertheless, faced with this sight and armed with the knowledge that I have, I in fact say 'I saw the bottle hit the floor and break', and not 'I saw the bottle break and hit the floor'. This is the form taken by the *normal* report; which is not in accord with either of the above *abnormal* possibilities, and which does not involve any form of temporal or temporal-narrative 'and'. For whether or not there is a presumption of ultimate temporal difference between the perceived events, there is no presumption of perception of that difference, and that which is reported is prefaced by 'I saw'; consequently the role of 'and' must be different. Its function is to separate, and preserve the direction of causality between, two causally related events.

(E) *The relation between the 'and' of causality and that of temporal narration.*

Remembering that these two 'ands' are not different senses, let us ask: how does the causal 'and' relate to that of temporal narration? But what does this mean? Consider: 'Potassium was added to the soil and the plants flowered'. This might occur in a mere temporally ordered list, or a list of causal relations, or a list of temporally ordered causal relations, 'and' being understood respectively as 'and then', 'and so', and 'and then as a result'. Then what temporal relations are entailed, where the assertion posits the events as extended and causally related? A complex disjunct of possible temporal relations is entailed, and this disjunct is logically equivalent to 'The beginning of flowering did not precede that of potassium addition'. This much can be logically extracted from the existence of a causal sequence. Yet since this proposition does not imply a relation of succession, the causal 'and' does not imply the 'and' of temporal narration. But it has temporal implications.

One is inclined to say that because one cannot have the beginning of an event without an event, the cause of the beginning and the event are one; whereas, paradoxically, the cause of an event and of its end are not one, even though the end is not separate from the event. This, however, is only sometimes true, depending on the *temporal properties* of the event. Compare 'He gave the ball a kick and it sailed away' with 'He shoved the piano and it moved'. The solid contact of a kick is over in a trice, but its effect lives on; and it cannot anticipate the contact with a pair of hands that will signal and cause its cessation. But only after some shoving would the piano budge, and only after more shoving acquire momentum sufficient to carry it on a little. Therefore the non-autonomous cause of its beginning to move is the shoving until that point, a phase of shoving, and of its movement is whatever shoving was responsible for its movement; and these are not identical. The overlapping extended cause of an extended event is not identical with the cause of its beginning. Moreover, this holds if the extended cause and extended effect are synchronous, though here the cause of the beginning of the effect is the beginning of the cause, and whereas in the previous case the non-autonomous phase could sometimes be isolated, it here makes no sense to speak of isolating the beginning of the cause. Consequently the distinction exists, but in different form, in the two cases. But if one extended event comes after another, whether touching at a temporal point or separated by a gap, no distinction can be drawn between the cause of an event and the cause of its beginning. Therefore, *whether* the distinction can be drawn at all, and *its very nature* when it can, depends not only on whether the events are extended, but also on whether they happen after one another, later than one another but not after, or synchronously.

People sometimes say that *a* and *b* being related as cause and effect has the temporal implication that *b* does not precede *a*. While this is true – supposed contrary examples are invariably psychological, under-described, mystery-mongering – the precise implication is that the beginning of *b* does not precede that of *a*. If this is disregarded, we might allow as temporally possible situations for causation the following: a cause happening either during or at the end of its effect, or later than, but not after it. But what in fact is temporally allowed by causation, and what not, depends on whether or not the events are extended temporally. Conversely, because a distinction can in some cases be drawn variously between the cause of an event and of its beginning, and in others not at all, the logical structure of the causal relation depends both on whether the events are extended, and on how they are placed temporally.

In sum. To say '*a* and *b*' does not, merely from its structure, tell us whether to understand this as '*a* and also under the same heading *b*', or '*a* and the next thing to happen was *b*', or '*a* and therefore *b*', or '*a* and then as a result *b*'. Which is the correct interpretation will depend on the nature of the linguistic enterprise, which is indicated by the temporal properties of events of kind *a* and *b*, together with our general knowledge of the existence of causal relations between events of this kind and of their temporal relations when causally related. Further, supposing the context to indicate that '*a* and *b*' is meant as '*a* and therefore *b*', the character of this 'therefore' is in the first place determined by the temporal properties of events of kinds *a* and *b*, and secondly determined as communication by common presumptions concerning the temporal placing of such events when causally related. Finally, supposing the context to make clear that '*a* and *b*' is meant as '*a* and therefore *b*', then what the temporal indications are, how *a* temporally stands to *b*, depends on whether or not they are temporally extended, and as a consequence of the above claims concerning the character of causation and its relation to time, depends in addition on the character of the causal bond.

V THE TEMPORAL ORDERING OF PSYCHOLOGICAL EVENTS

How do we order psychological events in the same person? Let us precede the discussion of this question by a discussion of the more fundamental question: how do we temporally *locate* psychological events? At first one is inclined to think that this is a matter which should await the findings of high-powered brain technologists – those Cartesian demons of contemporary philosophy! But there are reasons for resisting this view.

(A) *The perception of extensionless events.*

Consider, for example, the extensionless event of catching sight of something. Then if the perceived event is itself extensionless, the time of perception must be that of the event.

This, however, must be taken with a grain of salt, for the timing of physical events, but not of psychological, falls within the domain of physics. But if it takes one hundredth of a second for the requisite phenomena in the brain's visual centre to occur, must not perception occur at least one hundredth of a second after the event, and 'He saw it after it happened' always be true? But 'He saw it as it happened' is also true! Neither proposition denies the other, for they pass each other by like ships in the night. And the fact that perception is at least 10^{-2} seconds after the event does not land it in the domain of physics; for how would we precisely locate the time of perception? Given further necessary conditions of sight, we would advance the time of perception to some figure greater than 10^{-2} seconds after the event; but how could the precision applicable to these accumulated necessary conditions transfer on to perception, and what would constitute a termination of the above slide in time? Yet even if we could time the perception with infinite precision, this would not alter the timing as understood outside, and much of the time inside, the laboratory; for 'He saw it as it happened' does not imply simultaneity according to atomic clocks. Ordinarily we determine the time of events by reference to other events situated elsewhere in space, including the positioning of second hands on watches, which might be on one's wrist, which might in turn be a yard from one's eyes and five miles from the timed event.

If I speak of 'the time of physicists', then I do not mean anything other than time, for I want neither to divide time in two nor to thrust physicists into a transcendent realm. I refer rather to an order of measurement set up by those participating in a form of life where such orders of finesse have hitherto been absent; and I draw attention to the fact that the internal time experience of participants in that form of life could not accommodate these orders of measurement, for introduction of them must come from without and therefore fall outside the contents of the internal report. An instrument could inform him, but sight alone could not, that intervals of such order separated two perceived events. And yet if a physicist says, 'It has a half-life of 2.0003 hours', it is hours of which he speaks.

(B) *Catching sight of extended events: ordering through reaction.*

The position is different if the event is extended. If I witness the entire event, the time of perception is that of the event. But if one caught sight of it as it ran its course, two ways of locating the psychological event exist. I might identify its time with that of another event through *an impression* of simultaneity, as in 'As I caught sight of the building I saw a flash of lightning'. Alternatively, I might locate it through a first person report linking perception with a physical reaction, as in 'I jumped into the water the moment I saw her fall in'. These last cases are our prime concern.

In these cases we temporally relate the psychological event to a physico-psychological event, for the reaction to perception consists, not in movement, but the making of movement. One is inclined to say, first that movement can be timed with limitless precision, and secondly that the same must hold of making movement, since in any particular case their timing must be identical. But at microscopic level the limb seems to be in constant motion – and the same could be true of a rock – and there is no saying what counts as a beginning. Even if it was motionless, we could not prove that the first 10^{-3} seconds of subsequent motion was not involuntary motion. And even if we could time the act with limitless precision, this would not help us to do the same for perception, for we are not differentially aware of the first 10^{-3} seconds of the act and so able to say, 'That was the time of seeing'. All we could mean by 'I was aware of the first 10^{-3} seconds of the act' is 'There was a first 10^{-3} seconds of the act and I was aware of all the act'. Nor does it follow, if the act began at 2.0003 p.m. and I say 'I began to move as I caught sight of the ball', that I caught sight of it at 2.0003 p.m. (if I may be permitted the liberty of referring to the time of day by such a figure).

If we consider acts where one is unaware of the onset of action, as in 'I saw something near my face and found I had put up my hands', then while the beginning of action roughly indicates the time of perception, it cannot indicate relative temporal location. If the timing of psychological events is

162

through physical action, temporal order can be determined only if the time order is internally realized, which implies the existence of a report. But *ex hypothesi* there is none, and therefore all we can say is that the beginning of reactive action cannot have preceded perception. All we can then do is affirm the temporal implications of the explanatory 'and'.

In short, the following reasoning is not valid: at 2.0003 p.m. the lights went green, at 2.0003 p.m. his foot began pressing the accelerator, so in the same moment of time he saw the lights change and began pressing the accelerator; and therefore he could offer the following truthful first person report, 'In the same moment of time I saw the lights change and began pressing the accelerator', and we in turn affirm the corresponding proposition in the third person. For the above scientifically described physical facts are consistent with 'First I saw the lights change, then I pressed down', 'As I saw the lights change I began pressing down', 'I saw the lights change and (so) pressed down', and 'I saw the lights change and found I had pressed down'; *though hardly with 'I saw them change, hesitated, and then pressed down'*. And the same holds in the third person. Thus, where it is a question of a fraction of a second, it is a general truth that the time placing of sight and reaction within mind and consciousness *cannot be settled* by the methods of physics. (Therefore if I later say that in certain situations sight must precede response, this is consistent with *no* hesitation, from the point of view of a third person employing (mechanical) eyes and ears.)

(C) *Distinguishing internal order from impressions of order.*

It is paradoxical that an observer can say 'In the same moment he saw the lights change and began pressing down', in a statement that does not aim at being the third person proposition corresponding to the first person, while he himself says 'First I saw, then acted'. So we tend to treat first person ordering as an impression of an order ultimately determinable by modern physics, since this position appears to sidestep the difficulty. Yet, in fact, the internal order is the true order, and a true physicalism must match that order. But with unrelated internal events, the subjective order is an impression, and in certain cases the first person impressionistic report carries no special authority, for example, in the ordering of sight and act in 'I saw the lights change an instant after I began whistling'. Where we speak of internal order we mean something other than an impression; and both of these might be called forms of subjective order. How then does internal order differ from an impression of order? In that the true internal order is in all cases *ultimately settled* by the first person report.

The distinction is clearly visible in the following fact. It is not because we were aware of the perception at t' and the beginning of the act at t'', and t'' is later than t', that we report that reactive act follows perception. While this is a necessary condition of the truth of internal ordering, it is not what we would mention if asked to explain such ordering, by contrast with the ordering of unrelated psychological events through an impression of order. Internal ordering is nothing like an internal perception of time order, for our report, 'x and then y', does not derive from the fact that we are aware that our awareness of y was later than our awareness of x, even though it entails it. It derives, rather, from the fact that they are related to one another by more than the temporal relation, i.e. say by the relation of explicans to explicandum, or that of a slightly later shift to an earlier shift in a continuous process that still bears marks of passing through the earlier phase.

Internal temporal order is no myth. It is not realized through an impression; it is not the order of the scientists, even though physicalism must match this order; it is internal; it is geared to, but not reducible to, some form of explanatory order; it entails a temporal order in one's awareness, and an awareness of the temporal order of the awarenesses; and, finally, it must yet accord with such observed facts as the timing of the perceived effects of bodily movement.

VI THE TEMPORAL ORDERING OF PERCEPTION AND RESPONSE: (1) THE TRANSITION FROM THEIR SUBSUMPTIVE UNITY TO DIVERSITY

What temporal relation holds between perception and action deriving from perception? Consider the following set of cases.

(1) I look at a cup. As I look, I move my hand and take hold of the cup.

Here the later, but not the earlier, phase of looking is subordinated to reaching.

(2) I reach for a cup that lies just outside my visual field. Towards the end of this movement I am looking at the handle of the cup.

After but not before t'' I am reaching for what I see, and this is the later part of the act, both parts being joined in a subsumptive unity; and since this part is that between seeing and grasping, necessarily it begins as I see. We identify the moment of sight with the moment of the beginning of part of a continuous activity, neither through impression nor through interior report, but in logical consequence of the descriptions of acts. The moment of seeing *was* that of the ending of first part and the beginning of second, the two extended parts touch in time at that t'', and their relation is one of succession.

(3) I am walking towards a room to get an apple I left on the table. As I round the door I see the apple, walk towards it and get it.

Prior to and after t'' I head for the same object, yet from t'' I head for what I see. A new specification of my act is then open to me, having taken bearings in sight, for whereas I knew before where to go descriptively and practically, I now in addition know ostensively, i.e. I can now say 'I am aiming for that!' (pointing), aiming with hand and body for what lies in my visual field. A shift in the nature of what I am doing occurs at t'', and towards the end my movements are increasingly determined by *purely* visual data. Yet the terminus, in which the marriage of sight and movement is inextricably intimate, was projected as I set out in the other room.

Neither at nor immediately after t'' need I veer from the straight line I follow, so all that necessarily begins at t'' is that part of the act with a certain description, as in (2). Even if a movement to the right began at t'', we cannot with infinite exactitude identify this shift with the shift in sub-project. Apart from changing direction at t'', all that I initiated at t'' was the continuation of an act already projected to pass through this point; and I cannot play at being God and determine that these moments shall be identical. What is initiated at t'' is a non-autonomous part, a mere continuation of what is partly complete by t''; and so I initiate no new action at t''. Thus, we do not have here a case of coinciding of moment of sight and that of beginning of an act that stems from that sight. But this is the mythical beast we are stalking.

(4) I am looking down a shelf of books, alphabetically arranged, for a very familiar book which I know by sight and know to be there. I see it where I took it to be, and as I do I reach for it.

Looking for a book and reaching for it can, under this description, sometimes relate as in (1), where I look first and then reach for a cup (for recognition can take no time). I might even begin reaching as I begin looking, a looking whose sole function is to make possible the completion of reaching, looking and reaching being then subsumed under the heading of one act; whereupon the part of reaching following seeing necessarily dates from seeing. But sometimes I may look simply in order to be able to fetch, at my leisure so to speak; and then reaching dates from whatever instant I choose it shall.

(5) I am looking for the same book, in a haphazardly arranged array, and I do not even know if it is there. I catch sight of it and reach for it.

This is the point at which subsumptive unity changes to diversity.

While the first state of affairs, in (4), can hardly obtain here, the second can, for the whole procedure may crystallize into two distinct acts separated by an extensive delay. In any event, they *are* two, and this is of some importance; it is the moment of division. The nearest approximation to unification occurs, for example, in the situation in which one seeks the book in frantic and extremest haste, whereupon one's reaction to the sight of the book is like an exclamation, falling into a special class I shall later characterize. Let us christen such acts 'exclamatory acts'. For the moment, the temporal relation between search, sight and lunge is unclear; but nonetheless it is to me apparent that the lunge cannot be described as standing in a relation of succession to search and sight.

(6) I am looking to see if there are any interesting books on

166

a shelf, and I have agreed to point to those that I see. I catch sight of *The Charterhouse of Parma* and point to it.

This is the same as (5). For just as a title may take no time to recognize, so the recognition of an interesting book as interesting can occupy no time. Given my opinions and experience, for me to catch sight of the lettering *Anna Karenina* is immediately to see what immediately I see as interesting. 'Interesting' can in this respect be like a colour.

(7) I am looking for a book to read. I pass by a number of interesting books, but on catching sight of *The Charterhouse of Parma* I reach for it.

But 'a book to read' cannot be like a colour. (The puzzle with the exclamatory act is that it seems almost to be of that kind, as if the world gives one the kind of command one *of necessity* obeys.) Not because it may not be certain that I want to read it, but because to see it as to-be-read, in the sense I have in mind, is to see and in the instant decide. But this is not what I can *see*! Certainly I can see it as to-be-read in a variety of other senses: say as that which ought to be read by all, or as that which a moment ago I decided to read. But there is no seeing in a perception at t'' an intention formed by that perception to act as and from t''. I cannot recognize, almost as I can a colour, this dynamic mode of to-be-read. Objectification can go no further than the exclamatory act. Thereafter, externalization impoverishes internality beyond recognition.

(8) I am casually scanning a row of books in a shop. My reason is to see if there is anything interesting. One book interests me, and I reach for it.

VII THE TEMPORAL ORDERING OF PERCEPTION AND RESPONSE: (2) SNAP DECISIONS

(A) *Does time intervene between perceptions and resultant decisive actions?*

(9) I let my gaze roam down a row of books. My reason is more or less nothing: sheer curiosity. One book interests me, and I reach for it.

Something more than looking and reaching went on. I had the thought that the book was interesting; indeed, a whole train of thought might conceivably intervene, but at least I had that thought. This act is not exclamatory, nor is the response the later part of an act of which scanning is the earlier, so that these two activities fall apart and cannot be unified. So what alternative is there but to postulate an interval filled with thought? We can easily imagine such a state of affairs, of course, in which I ruminate at length about the virtues of a book, decide to look at it and reach for it; but is some interval of thought essential? Need there be a temporal interval between catching sight of and beginning to reach in a case in which one reports, 'I saw, thought "What a wonderful book it is!", decided to look at it and reached for it'? Now I say that thought occurs, for the reason that having the thought 'What a wonderful book it is!' is more than recognizing the presence of an interesting book, and also because it is in the light of this consideration that one embarks upon action; and what functions as reason for a novel act that is not exclamatory must enter the mind as thought. Further, I report my thoughts as: 'What a wonderful book it is! I think I'll have a look at it'. Then cannot the thought be synchronous with the sight, and the decision with the thought, and the beginning of act with the decision? Might sight, thought, decision, beginning to act, all be crammed into the same extensionless instant, and yet sight lead to thought, thought to decision, decision to beginning to act?

Let me review the position. At t' I catch sight of a book with title X, and I think 'What a wonderful book it is!', and reach for it. This description so far fits both the case of exclamatory act, which we will discuss later, and 'snap' decision, which is our present concern. Then is there an interval between catching sight of and beginning to act? Does the thought come after the sight, the decision after the thought, and beginning to act after the decision?

What is deciding? To decide to act is to resolve to act, to accept the truth of the practical proposition, 'I shall act'. It need not terminate indecision, for indecision is the state of being unable as yet to accept that proposition as either true or false, and its acceptance need not be preceded by uncertainty. 'He decided' need not be understood to report a successful conclusion of an active process of practical deliberation called 'trying to make up his mind'. Whereas 'He was trying to make up his mind' reports activity, 'He decided' does not. If a man is voluntarily trying to do *x*, and does it, voluntarily he did *x*; but if he is voluntarily trying to decide, and does, then although he *freely* decided he did not *voluntarily* decide: *x* was something he was trying to do, but decide was not, for there is an activity of *x*-ing but none of deciding. Therefore 'he decided' need not report successful termination of actively trying to decide, and cannot report an act, extended or extensionless. Nor can we necessarily place the necessary prior state of non-decision as being at least in part between sight and act. For although the practical question only dates from seeing, it is not clear whether it ever arose as a question in the mind of the agent.

We must therefore reject the above two spurious ways of proving the necessary presence of an interval between sight and act, viz. that which argues from the supposed presence of a preceding process of attempting to make up one's mind, and that which argues from the prior obtaining of a state of non-decision. That process need not take place, since indecision need not obtain, and the transition from non-decision to decision need not be sandwiched between seeing and deciding, since the question need not have arisen.

Must not decision proceed then out of that sector of non-decision that dates from seeing, for does not the decision relate to what is given in perception, i.e. the book *X*? Does it not arise out of that perception? For it is not the book *X* given in the abstract, but in perception concretely present, to which one relates in this decision; and it is moreover because it is thus concretely presented that one decides. So must not there be an interval between the presenting of *X* concretely through perception to the awareness of the subject, and the decision to reach for the *X* thus presented?

(B) *The unification of non-autonomous part-events*

Let me express the problem facing us in this present Section,

VII(B), by comparing objects and sounds. In a number of senses of 'part', objects can have parts, and amongst these senses is that of autonomous part-objects, exemplified in examples like nibs and tyres. While we cannot assume that events have parts in the way objects do, nevertheless we *do* unify some, but not other, events or phenomena under the heading of single complex events. For example, the sound of footsteps is not one complex sound but a characteristic arrangement of distinctive sounds, whereas a second-long burst of sound from a motorbike is both one sound of a certain kind and constituted of perhaps a dozen bangs. Again, while ten repeated continuous clangs count as ten sounds *and not also* as one complex sound, if all hitting on wood caused a brief clang that instantly turned into a brief honk, say over a mere second, then we might well consider this *a type* of sound that we can thereafter elsewhere both independently identify and analyse. Thus, the problem is to know, given two sounds of determinate kind, whether or not we may say that together they constitute a third sound. Speaking more generally, what is it that enables us to confer on some autonomous events the further title of part-event of a more complex event?

If a magnet needle, a, moves at t' through pushing, while magnet needle, b, moves at t' through attraction to a, then these events are two and distinct, even though simultaneous and causally related. Their distinctness follows from the distinctness of their causes, for two non-distinct part-events must share the same distinct cause, though they need not share the same non-distinct cause. This criterion of identity enables us simultaneously to characterize them as part-events and to unify them, in cases where the question of autonomy is an issue. Distinctness follows also from the fact that there is no concept, c, analogous to 'the movement of a dumb-bell' as opposed to 'movement of a binary star', instances of which encompass such events as movement of a or b as parts of itself, and provide a concept under which autonomous events of the kind of the unified part-events can be counted.

But if I depress end a of a see-saw, the movement of end a did not cause that of the other end, b, and both have as cause my pushing at a; for these movements are non-autonomous part-events, merely differentiated elements in the autonomous event of see-saw movement caused by the autonomous event of pushing. All diverse events necessarily encompass such part-events, encompassed under the heading of the concept of events of the kind of the autonomous event, and, as an example of the non-diverse, I suggest the momentary appearance of a faint star, of any or indeterminate colour. But the kind of part-event varies, for whereas end movement (say the end of a see-saw) necessitates object movement of that see-saw, a phase of object movement (say the first slow phase of an avalanche) or else a simple harmonic wavering motion (say the sway of the hips of a walking woman) could have occurred on their own. And because a distinct phenomenon could thereby cause wavering in an advancing object, it follows that one could have a distinct cause of the wavering of a wavering advancing object; but this one could not have in the case of end movement. Yet even where a distinct cause is a theoretical possibility, there may not be one, since the events may share the one cause and be encompassed under a unifying concept. The immediate consequence of this is that the potentially distinct event disappears, as a non-distinct but autonomous part-event, into the event that is the effect of the distinct cause of that non-distinct event.

This becomes apparent in the following examples. (1) Impact with a moving tennis racket at t' causes a tennis ball to pass from p' to p'', over time interval t' to t'', while continuous air turbulence causes wavering between t' and t''. Therefore although wavering and advance are integrated under 'movement of the ball between t' and t'''', and are thus potentially merely part-events of a single event, here they are each autonomous *and* distinct; for their causes differ, they merely coincidentally occupy the same time, and each could occur in isolation. (2) Impact with a racket causes both advance and wavering, and so causes wavering advance. Therefore these events are neither autonomous nor distinct, for they are integrated under 'movement of the ball between t' and t'''', they are simultaneous and they share the one cause. Contrast in this respect a girl whose walk is naturally sinuous with one in which sinuosity is artificially contrived: the former engages in one activity, the latter in two. (3) A top-spin shot in tennis – and here we merely characterize a variant of (2) – combines advance of the ball from p' to p'' through thrust at t', with revolution from t' to t'' through friction at t'. But because these causes are non-autonomous part-events of the autonomous event of impact, so analogously are the differentiated part-events of the ball's movement non-autonomous. Thus we introduce differentiation into the cause in order differentially to explain differentiated elements of its effect, linear and angular motion, yet without positing these differentiated elements as distinct events.

To describe the movement of magnet b as 'movement of one half of a binary magnet' is not, as it is with describing end movement as 'movement of a see-saw' or angular movement as 'movement of a ball', to identify the autonomous event whose cause causally explains a supposed non-autonomous movement of b. Because the cause of movement of b is not that of movement of a, these two events cannot be encompassed by any third event, c, as its parts. While movement of a hammer-head can be subsumed under 'movement of a hammer', and magnet b might similarly have been a mere part of a unifying totality, in fact it is not. When we think about this question we are constantly inclined to fragment objects into so many parts thrusting one against another, but the cost of doing so is the expulsion of solidity and force from the universe.

Consequently, if we are to unify two events, a and b, as part-events of an autonomous event, we must discover such an event, c, related to a and b as follows. (1) c constitutively and non-causally explains a and b, (2) *vice versa* in the reverse sense, (3) the cause of c and a and b is one and the same autonomous event, (4) the occurrence of events of kind c requires such elements as a and b as differentiated elements of itself, and (5) the concept, c, establishes a principle for counting events.

(C) *The attempted unification of perceptions and derivative thoughts*

It is suggested that the following events might each stem

172

from one another and yet occur at the same instant: catching sight of X (SX), having the thought that X has property p (θXp), deciding to act upon X (DX), and acting upon X (AX).

Consider the relation between SX and θXp (through SX). We distinguish 'θXp while SX', which records an impression of simultaneity, from 'θXp through and while SX', which is merely contentious. But the latter cannot record an impression of simultaneity, for since in 'θXp through and while SX' the thought both stems from the presence of the object in the visual field and posits its object as ostensively before the mind, it follows that the report of simultaneity cannot be of a mere impression.

Yet what could constitute the basis of such a non-impressionistic report? Hitherto, as in (1) to (4) in Section VI, we have employed identity considerations in deriving such reports. For this reason we seek a unifying concept, c, which will unite under that heading, as non-autonomous part-events, SX and θXp that is through SX. One is strongly inclined to turn to the concept, seeing-as, since it seems closely to match the specification: θXp through and while SX. Yet in fact it does not.

It is true that if one sees X as having property p, in some senses of 'see as', this entails seeing X and taking X to have property p; and if the sense of 'see as' makes of it a content of consciousness, the taking of X to have property p must itself take such an occurrent form as thinking. But to see X as having property p is not to have the thought that it does, even though looking at X and thinking perhaps complicated thoughts about its being p entails that one sees X as having the property, for the reverse entailment does not hold; and nothing could make of θXp a non-autonomous event. Nor could SX be either non-autonomous or a non-autonomous part-event of seeing X as having property p, any more than the movement of the earlier-mentioned magnet could disappear under the lid, 'movement of binary magnet'. Therefore we do not have to distinguish 'seeing X as p' (SX as p), from the contentious 'θXp through and while SX' by such an intuitive idea as that in the latter case the thought would be detached from the object, floating as it were above it, whereas the seen-as property would be unified with its object, almost as a smile is on a face. It follows that seeing-as is not that unifying concept, c.

The non-impressionistic report of simultaneity must be based on considerations of identity, since the merely explanatory 'and' (or 'through') does not necessitate simultaneity (for on this question the explanatory 'and' is silent). Yet there is no concept that relates to SX and θXp in the way required to constitute an identifying heading. The nearest approximation is that of seeing-as, but this does not encompass the thought as a non-autonomous part-event. Therefore the description of θXp as 'θXp through and while SX' must be incoherent, if identity is the ground of the report of simultaneity. For since the 'through' is not that encountered in 'end b of the see-saw moved through movement of end a', events θXp and SX must be distinct, even though lodged in a non-impressionistic report of simultaneity, and this contradicts the supposition of identity.

Consequently, the report 'SX and θXp' is to be taken either as implying temporal progression, and expanded into the narrative 'I saw X and then thought θXp', or else as a merely explanatory report with a merely explanatory 'and' employed in 'SX and θXp'. This latter, while consistent with 'and then', does not necessitate its use (unless it misreports a seeing-as, in which case it is a different situation).

(D) *The form of unity holding between activity and subordinated perception*

At t' SX; and AX through DX through θXp through SX. Then suppose we call the time of beginning AX, t_a, and the seeing of X at t_a, S_aX. The question is, whether t' and t_a, and SX and S_aX are identical.

How do AX and S_aX relate? Here are two events. One at least of them is distinct from the pair of events, SX and θXp, whose relation we have just examined. Both of them can simultaneously possess consciousness in some measure. And clearly they stand to one another in a relation of some intimacy. But what is that relation? *Ex hypothesi* their times are one, namely t_a. At t_a I initiate an act in which looking plays a functional role. For *reaching* entails that one posits its object as existing, and at a known place, since throughout reaching one aims one's hand at that object. Also, whereas *looking at one's left hand* is functionless and floats clear of the simple deed of laying one's right hand on one's left, for here the necessary putative knowledge is previsual, *looking at the object of reaching* characteristically plays a functional role in reaching. While I might first look and then reach without looking, this is not usual, partly because it would often issue in a mere groping around, partly because it would often result in an act the precise instant of whose termination lay beyond my control. And while this latter fact will not matter in touching a nearby wall, it matters greatly in reaching forward to take hold of a precious and fragile glass. Coordination of simultaneous hand and finger movement generally necessitates the use of sight. And even where it is inessential to the performance of the act, it is essential to the inessential but nonetheless real aiming at a point, and thus essential to the chosen form taken by the act. But sometimes there is nothing to which it is essential.

The object given to sight through action, and thus to action through sight, appears in consciousness under a dual banner. It is not merely that such an object is an object both of act and of looking. For it may in the first place be present to consciousness only through sight, as in skirting an obstacle, and secondly be capable of completion only through continuous looking, as in reaching for a fragile glass or catching a ball. While it is an open question through what channel putative knowledge of position comes, that putative knowledge is a logically necessary condition of reaching. Nor is this knowledge characteristically cast in non-ostensive propositional form, for while I may know where a speck on this page is situated, and that simply through seeing it, I do not need to be able to *state* its exact whereabouts without further looking, but need merely to be able to see, or point at, or touch it. Moreover, as I reach to touch it, the continuously changing relative position of speck and finger is given solely through sight, and once again is not cast in non-ostensive propositional form.

I give, therefore, an ostensive characterization of the act I initiate at t_a. I say, 'I began reaching for that X', pointing in

175

the sight of those with sight to what lies in all our visual fields. Yet the act *is* a *reaching for a particular object*, and that the object is given to the act through sight, either at or before its beginning or before its completion, does not enter the description of either object or act. Nevertheless the act involves the use of sight, since I bring together hand and object *through* bringing them together in my visual field. While it need not have been so, it is in fact the case. Sight is here my immediate mode of access to the non-bodily reality, and thus to the relation of the bodily and non-bodily that I am concerned actively to modify.

Some kind of unity exists here between looking and reaching. In the final instant of conjunction of hand and object is celebrated the ultimate unity of the motor and visual worlds. Then is looking a component activity of reaching – as gear-changing is of driving, as the angular motion of a tennis ball is of its movement? The listening to music by a practising ballerina is subordinated to, but not a constitutive component of, her dancing. By 'subordinated' we mean that her occupation is dancing, not listening, and that she is listening because dancing, and not vice versa. So it is with reaching for a book: looking is subordinated to, but not a part of reaching, even when it plays an essential functional role. One has merely to remember *what* it is that is done, the bringing of one's hand to an object, to realize this. That the object comes to consciousness solely through sight does not make of it any the less a determinate particular object. This holds even in pointing at an after-image!

It is because one is engaged in reaching, then, that one engages in whatever functionally essential looking is subordinated to that reaching. Whatever brings about that reaching must bring about subordinated looking. For example, if the desire to please causes dancing, it must cause any subordinated listening. Consequently, if SX causes AX, it must cause any subordinated looking at X during AX, L_aX. But at this point two arguments, both designed to demonstrate that $SX \neq S_aX$ and therefore that there exists a time-interval between the two, emerge as invalid. (1) Because L_aX is subordinated to AX, L_aX and AX are one; and because L_aX entails S_aX at t_a, S_aX and AX are one. Therefore whatever causes AX causes

S_aX, and SX and S_aX therefore are distinct. Then, since SX and S_aX are distinct points in the single continuous process of looking at X, an interval of time must separate SX and S_aX, and therefore separate SX and AX. (2) Because L_aX is subordinated to AX, whatever causes AX causes L_aX. And because L_aX entails S_aX, whatever causes AX causes S_aX. Therefore if SX causes AX it causes S_aX, and therefore SX and S_aX must be distinct and temporally apart.

Argument (1) is invalid because 'subordinated to' does not mean 'constitutive of'. This implies that we cannot say that listening or looking are constitutive of practising or reaching, but rather that *through* performing one activity one was enabled to perform another. It is invalid because we cannot infer from the fact that SX causes L_aX that it causes S_aX, since t_a need not be the first moment of L_aX; and even if it were, S_aX might have a different cause. Argument (2) is invalid for the latter two reasons. For all that we can know of L_aX is that it is subordinated to (some at least end) part of AX. Therefore the looking at t_a need not be subordinate.

Nevertheless at t_a I initiate an act of which I must be able to give the ostensive characterization: 'I began reaching for that X'. I act under this heading, rather than under one cast in terms of coordinates; for at t_a I already project an act which involves in its concluding phase the inextricably intimate marriage of sight and gesture. Therefore at t_a the object of aiming-through-looking is given already as the goal-through-looking. Then is such seeing distinct from AX? But an AX involving a subordinated L_aX need not involve S_aX at t_a. Yet if S_aX exists, X must of necessity be given in S_aX at t_a as the goal-through-looking.

(E) *Unity and disunity in the mind*

The unity between S_aX and AX, apparent in the description of X in S_aX as the goal-through-looking, is neither that of identity nor that which holds between L_aX and AX, the unity of subordination. For the unity of S_aX and the beginning of AX is not such that they can be joined under the one concept and stand revealed as differential elements of the one event, which emerges in the fact that there is no presumption that

S_aX and the beginning of AX share a cause. Through the very same fact it also emerges that the unity cannot be that of subordination.

But that the unity of L_aX and AX, the unity of subordination, is not that of identity, is less obvious. After all, if L_aX has a cause then AX shares it, and this seems to prepare the way for the unity of identity. But under what concept could L_aX and AX be unified? Either under AX or none! AX entails putative knowledge, and L_aX provides that knowledge; but while the property of being putatively located is a logically necessary condition of being an object of reaching, reaching consists in no more than advancing one's hand towards an object with the intention of grasping it. Thus, reaching does not incorporate into itself the knowledge that makes itself possible. How could such an advancing-towards, informed by such an intention, incorporate anything more than such phenomena as an intended wavering or revolving? And there is no further and wider concept, analogous to the concept of movement that can but need not incorporate angular motion, that could unite the two activities. All one could appeal to is the concept of occupation; but reaching *is* one's occupation.

Consequently, we cannot incorporate either S_aX or L_aX under AX, even though any cause of L_aX will be the cause of AX. Despite the fact that they share causes, that they are unified and that AX and not L_aX is the occupation, they cannot be unified into a single activity under the heading, 'occupation'. Now within certain limits a man can have a number of distinct occupations: he may walk, whistle and think, and no unity need exist here. The mind can be occupied simultaneously by several motor activities, walking and whistling; by several perceptual activities, looking where he is going and scanning the landscape; and simultaneously by thinking. While some of these will on occasion be subordinated to one another, on other occasions they will not, and in either situation the separate or united activities can remain distinct. But the activity of gear-changing is not distinct from driving, and neither is the activity of revolving one's hand as one reaches to catch something which is itself revolving a distinct activity from that of reaching. All of these relations are possibilities. The activities can change their status too: the intent driver slows down, continues to look where he is going, but now begins to inspect the landscape and to think about it: the ballerina dancing as she listens becomes a ballerina who listens as she dances. And so on.

A man looking at a row of books may be walking, his walking distinct from but subordinated to his looking; and simultaneously he may be thinking about what he sees. Then whereas the subject-matter of his thinking is provided by sight, neither thinking nor looking are subordinated to one another, for neither is the purpose behind the other. Then at t' he sees X, and his thoughts swerve in a new direction, and he continues looking at X, and perhaps his walking comes to a halt. The cessation of walking is subordinated, if at all, to looking, but neither looking nor thinking are subordinated to one another. At t_a a new motor activity of reaching commences, and from t_a onwards looking at X may be subordinated to reaching, and is certainly so subordinated some time before the end of reaching. Now it is possible that he reaches with such avidity that his thinking dissolves into the intent activity of reaching, only to resume in a moment. Then, in that case, all of his faculties, his whole self, are just prior to the moment of contact joined together in a tight and focused unity, albeit a unity falling short of identity. A moment later a partial loss of this unity may come into being in the form of novel activities: say, humming to himself together with the unique activity of thinking. This continual focusing and unfocusing, intent engagement followed by partial disengagement, is characteristic of consciousness.

That is the position as I see it. It follows that if we are to demonstrate the existence of a slice of time between SX and AX, we must do so by discovering two moments of differing content falling under the heading of the same process-activity. From this alone it will follow that they are temporally apart. But how can we demonstrate that t' is not t_a, that the instant of catching sight is not that of beginning to reach? Not by indicating that the content of motor activity at t' and t_a differ, for walking may continue without being subordinated to reaching, and reaching is a novel act at t_a. Not by indicating a different perceptual content, for though X is seen at t_a as the goal-through-looking, we have no way that is not circular of characterizing how X is seen at t' unless we consider θXp and DX. The difficulty stems from the fact that SX and AX are distinct, and from the fact that L_aX and AX are two distinct activities. Were it not for the insertion of a developmental thought process, no proof could be forthcoming – as we shall see when we consider the exclamatory act. But whereas the body is a thing of many parts, the mind is not; and whereas consciousness can simultaneously accommodate a number of distinct, or else differentially different but not distinct activities, *the line of thinking* cannot analogously fragment into a number of distinct and separate activities, even though it is an *intermittent* thread.

Consequently, since θXp is not identical with DX (on the basis of θXp), it follows that these mental events are temporally apart. This conclusion would follow even if thinking could so fragment at any instant, for the above distinct events occur within the one process-activity. But since SX is no later than θXp, and DX no later than the beginning of AX, SX and AX must be temporally apart.

The whole difficulty arises out of the fact that *we are trying to discover the temporal relation between two points in two distinct but intersecting processes.* This in turn derives from the fact that a variety of distinct and not necessarily unified processes and activities can possess the mind at any particular instant. If all of the latter could be united and ultimately identified even though differentiated, if division and fragmentation were not possible within the mind, the problem of temporal ordering would be readily resoluble and no such philosophical difficulties as have exercised us in this paper would arise. Thus, because θXp and DX (through θXp) occur within the same process and are distinct events, it is possible for us to say 'θXp and then DX' – as indeed we do say! But only if there exists such an intervening thought process between SX and AX can we pass from the fact that AX stems from SX to the claim that AX follows SX, and report 'SX and then AX'. Otherwise, all that we say is 'SX and AX', employing the 'and' of explanation. *It is the intersection of one distinct process with another, where the content at a point in one leads to shift in the other, that creates the difficulty.* For example, a looking which is distinct from, and perhaps not unified with, motor activity may bring to consciousness a perceptual content that is the explanation of a shift in motor activity, or of the inception of an entirely new motor activity. In the present case under discussion, case (9), distinctness must obtain, say that of SX and the beginning of AX, or SX and θXp; for distinctness is guaranteed simply through the fact that these events are integrated into distinct processes. Because numerous processes and activities can simultaneously fill consciousness, any point in one must be distinct from any point in another, and the temporal implication of their distinctness is no more than can be extracted from the use of the explanatory 'and'. Because these processes are not all unified in such a way that they emerge as mere diversities within the one process, the problem of temporal ordering is acute. Events within distinct unrelated processes are temporally ordered through impression; events within the one process are ordered under the heading of the unifying concept; and events within processes related in subordination can be derivatively ordered in the latter fashion. But where an event in the subordinate process leads to a shift in the other, all that we can say by way of temporal ordering is whatever the explanatory 'and' permits. Now it is the presence of the intervening unitary thought-process that enables us in this present case to establish the existence of a time difference between two events in distinct processes, SX and the beginning of AX, so that SX and AX are joined by an 'and' that is at once explanatory and mediately so.

VIII CONCLUSION

(A) *The exclamatory act*

(Resuming the numeration employed at the beginning of Section VI)

    (10) A man is about to cross a road. He turns his head and sees a bus thirty yards away. He steps back a pace or so, taking his time about it.

(11) The bus is ten yards away: he jumps back (he is beginning to take *its* time about it!).

(12) It is five yards away: he hurls himself back.

(13) It is a mere two yards away: he topples back wildly out of the way.

(14) He is walking alone in the country. He suddenly sees something near his face and gives a start of avoidance.

(15) The room is suddenly lit by a brilliant flash. He jumps.

There is no difference between (10) and (9), which we have discussed at length; and (15) is the case of shock, which we do not discuss in this paper. The exclamatory act occurs between (11) and (14), and the purest example is probably (12).

In (12) we say, 'He saw it and leaped back'. The correct description cannot situate the expressions, 'and then', or 'at the same time', before 'he leaped back'. I say neither, 'He saw the bus a few yards away and then hurled himself back', nor 'As he hurled himself back he caught sight of the bus', nor 'At the same moment in time he caught sight of the bus and hurled himself back', nor 'As he caught sight of the bus he began to hurl himself out of the way', nor 'At the same moment in time he began to hurl himself out of the way and caught sight of the bus'.

We have attempted to lay bare the rationale that underlies these linguistic and conceptual facts. Without that rationale we could do no more than appeal to a compound of ear and intuition, and that is no more than a guide that can help us retain our sense of reality. Indeed, it is through a consideration of the rationale that we come to be sure as to what we do and do not say, in the most proper sense of those words, and a union is forged between our practical capacities with certain concepts and our theoretical understanding of these concepts. But despite these qualifications, it seems to me nonetheless to be true that one's linguistic ear is an important piece of philosophical laboratory equipment.

In describing the situation in (12) the participant might insist on one rather than another order of words. For example, if he is explaining his behaviour, he says, 'I saw the bus and hurled myself out of the way'. This is the explanatory 'and'.

From our earlier discussion we see that the above preference of order does not result from a merely suspected temporal order. Further, we see that all that follows temporally is that one's catching sight of the bus cannot have happened after hurling or beginning to hurl oneself out of the way. It is not that there *might be some time* between seeing and hurling, or that there *might be none*: when we say that the explanatory 'and' is silent on these particular orderings, we simply mean that such questions cannot arise here. In short, it is a kind of temporal Indeterminacy Principle.

(B) *The causal implications of temporal separateness**

Why, in (9), did SX not cause AX? Because AX was only mediately related to SX and separated from it by an interval of time, so that whatever settled that AX should occur happened in that interval. We do not believe in causation over a gulf of time in the mind, and know in any event that θXp and DX settled the matter.

But had he not seen X, AX would not have occurred, and is not this grounds for describing SX as the cause of AX? It might conceivably be taken as grounds for supposing, not that SX causes AX, but that it is one of a set of causes of AX. But even this cannot be true, for if we do not believe in action-at-a-distance-in-time in the mind, we must situate all contributory causes at no distance in time from the effect, which here begins at t_a; whereas the time of SX is t', for SX is the extensionless event of catching sight of, and t' is other than t_a.

But we need not even invoke any such principle as the unacceptability of action-at-a-distance-in-time in the mind. For it is clear that if SX, which occurs at t', contributes to the occurrence of AX, which begins at the later t_a, it must be through the knowledge acquired in SX of the presence and position of X, KX. This knowledge, which is that without which AX would not have occurred, was acquired at t', for it comes from and with SX: we do not need to keep looking at X to continue to know that X stands before us, and it is

---

* I should like to emphasize, what I mention in the first paragraph of this paper but fail to mention here and in VIII(C), that, unless expressly indicated, wherever I here speak of *causation* I have in mind *immediate causation*.

the discovery of its proximity and position which is that without which AX would not have occurred. Now SX happens at and is done by t', being the extensionless event of catching sight of, and so is distinct from the relevant phase (lasting from t_a until the end of AX) of the enduring state of knowledge of presence and position that contributes to the performance of AX. We can hardly say *simpliciter*, 'AX because SX', for this 'because' works only on the assumption that one remembers what one discovered through SX. It follows that SX can contribute to the occurrence of AX only through the mediation of KX. Therefore SX can neither cause nor be a contributory cause of AX.

How then does SX relate to this knowledge, KX, that was necessary for the beginning and completion of AX? At t' SX happens, at t_a AX begins, at $t_{a+\epsilon}$ AX ends. It is at t' that knowledge of the presence and position of X is acquired. This same knowledge – as we say – plays a role in the genesis and perpetuation of AX. Now without prejudice as to status, let us call the knowledge concerning X that one has at the above times, 'K', 'K_a' and '$K_{a+\epsilon}$'. Are these one? That is to say, when we speak of these instances of knowledge, are we speaking of temporal instantiations of the one enduring state? I think we are. For at t' an event happens, the acquisition of knowledge, and what was acquired endures, for it was at t' that one acquired the knowledge that one has at t_a (etc.). This means that KX, the knowledge of presence and position of X, has not been acquired a second time since t'; so it is not merely that *what* is known at t' and *what* known at t_a (etc.) are one, but that *a single state* has endured. Knowledge, a state, endures of necessity for some time, and contingently KX endures from t at least as far as $t_{a+\epsilon}$. Therefore, since KX begins at t' it is necessary that it endure for some time beyond t', while it is contingent that the KX at t_a (etc.) is an instantiation of the state that commenced at t'. And yet in fact it is.

In any event, a necessary requirement of catching sight of, of noticing, something is that the acquired knowledge concerning the item shall endure for however small a time, for perception is discerned through a shift in report, or response, or both. We need not therefore assume that knowledge of necessity endures, though it does. How then does SX relate to K' and K_a? SX at t' entails K', since SX is a noticing and therefore a registering of X's presence and position. But SX cannot cause K', for that which *is* a noticing-of-presence-of could not cause a simultaneous knowledge-of-presence-of.

Can SX cause K_a? We must first discover in what other relations SX stands to K_a. Not in a relation of entailment, despite the fact that K' and K_a are temporal instantiations of the one enduring state and the fact that SX entails K'. The necessary endurance of the state of knowledge, KX, an endurance that necessarily carries it beyond t', provides no *a priori* measure of the extent of that endurance. It is for this reason that the non-distinctness of SX and K', together with the fact that K' and K_a are united in the manner indicated, do not jointly entail that SX and K_a are one. After all, SX happens at t', whereas K_a obtains at t_a. It follows that we cannot argue from the fact that SX cannot cause K' to the claim that it cannot cause K_a – if our grounds are that SX cannot be distinct from K_a. Yet it does in fact follow for different reasons. Neither SX itself nor its supposed cause can explain the persistence of KX to whatever point it endures, including t_a, and this holds no matter how brief that endurance. How could light rays, or the sight of someone's face, explain why that sight lives on in my memory? My claim is consistent with the fact that SX entails some endurance of KX, howsoever small, for if it is a fact that whenever SX occurs there must be that which is other than SX to explain the persistence of KX to whatever point it persists to, it follows that a necessary condition of SX is the presence of that which will explain its persistence to some point or another. This does not specify how long KX will endure, nor does it say that it is already settled at t' how long it will endure, nor is it inconsistent with there being a shifting multiplicity of explanatory factors. But SX cannot then be the explanation of the fact that KX endures up until the later point, t_a. SX explains the knowledge, knowledge that endures up until that point, but not the endurance of the knowledge. So if SX non-causally explains the knowledge, K', and if something other than SX explains, not merely that the knowledge persists beyond t', but its persistence to whatever point it does persist to, how could SX causally explain the existence of a state of knowledge concerning X at any time, including t_a? Given the above two explanatory devices, nothing else requires explanation.

An interval characteristically intervenes between SX and the beginning of AX; temporal indeterminacy is the result of attempting to abolish this interval. For these reasons no such thing exists as a clear-cut example of action being immediately caused by sight, and characteristically and by nature sight does not immediately cause action. If we are considering the situation where an interval of time separates the sight and the onset of action, the following are ways of driving the above point home. First, it is KX and not SX that contributes to both the genesis and the perpetuation of AX. Secondly, SX does not even cause that which is its own contribution to AX, namely KX, and this is so whether the time be the beginning, middle or end of AX, for it causes neither K_a, $K_{a+\frac{\epsilon}{2}}$, nor $K_{a+\epsilon}$. Therefore SX is not even related to AX through a mediate causal relation.

(C) *The causal implications of temporal indeterminacy*

Requirements of space necessitate my making short work of this Section. In any event, this paper addresses itself primarily to questions of timing in the mind, with these additional complicated matters no more than barely in view.

My claim is not that exclamatory acts are 'really' of the kind of (9). I do not wish to claim that because SX does not in (9) cause AX, catching sight of a bus cannot cause the response of hurling oneself out of the way. Rather is it as follows: that whereas, on the one hand, the shock (15) involves immediate causation of a kind, and whereas in (9) on the other hand SX does not cause AX, example (10) lies along part of the spectrum that lies between these cases. Because in the shock the start is not an action – and the perception a pretty poor and primitive example of the species – the situation of (10) along such a spectrum is of vastly more moment that the mere making of a claim that it falls between these two cases. For my suggestion is not that nothing in consciousness can have a cause, but rather than perceptions do not immediately cause actions. But if such a case as (10) cannot provide us with a clear and unambiguous example of such causation, where shall we turn to discover one? Thus, to demonstrate that (10) is a true intermediate case between these other cases is tantamount to showing the impossibility of such causation.

But this last has not, after all, been demonstrated. Because the arguments which seem to me to do so are lengthy and complicated, I had better let the matter rest at this stage. I must also point out that I have been discussing actions of which one is fully conscious: actions of which one is barely aware raise many new questions. So, to a lesser extent, do habitual actions.

II

BERNARD WILLIAMS

I have found O'Shaughnessy's paper very interesting, but also difficult. I shall not approach its position head-on, and I shall have to omit many important points. I shall confine myself to some critical remarks and questions on five separate points.

(1) This is not a central issue. On pp. 145-6 O'Shaughnessy says: 'In general perception requires the simultaneous presentation of the simultaneous as simultaneous, and as simultaneous with that presentation': a condition which is explicated in the following terms, that for some x, we experience at x a and b, and for some y, a and b happen at y, and for some z, we experience a and b as happening together at z, and $x=y=z$.

My question is: what is the third condition over and above the first two? If there is an independent third condition here, then it must be possible for it to fail independently. In how many ways, then, can it fail to be the case that a and b are experienced as happening together, granted that they are indeed experienced as happening? First, we may experience at different moments their happening; this is failure of the first condition. Second, we may experience at the same moment their happening, but know that they happen in fact at different moments (as with astronomical events, etc.), and use this knowledge to 'correct' our experiences; this is failure of the second condition. Distinctive failure of the third condition, then, would require this possibility: that we experience at the same moment things that indeed happen at the same moment, but look (or sound) as though they happened at different moments. If it is indeed a *phenomenological* fact that we experience them at the same moment, which I take to be O'Shaughnessy's intention, then it is obscure to me what can be understood by this third possibility. The only thing that occurs to me as a putative example of it would be a case in which the coexperienced events contained features indicative of objective non-simultaneity, such as different clock-readings; but in fact (the second condition being satisfied) these indications were erroneous – at least one of the clocks was wrong, they were in different time zones, etc. But this possibility introduces too shallow a sense of 'its looking as though they were non-simultaneous' to give any real content to the distinctive failure of the third condition, and hence to the third condition. All this introduces is a particular subclass of happenings, and in particular of simultaneities (of clock-readings and other events), which are relevant to inference about the satisfaction of the second condition. Hence, though it is a puzzling matter, I am not yet convinced that O'Shaughnessy has really got three conditions here, and not merely two.

(2) I take it to be one of O'Shaughnessy's main points that psychological order, and internal process related to that, just cannot in principle, and for conceptual reasons, be precisified beyond a certain point in accordance with the demands of a physical accuracy applied to physical events. This is not just a matter of *ignorance*. Hence (in his view) some conditions of a causal account of connections between certain supposedly temporally contiguous items – perception and action – cannot be met. I think his first claim may well be true, though I shall disagree with a couple of his arguments for it. With regard to his conclusion, I am not sure either that it follows or that it is true.

On p. 163, he discusses the relations between, on the one hand, the objectively determinable time relations between a perceptual stimulus and the (physical) external beginning of physical action and, on the other hand, the internal psychological order; and he says that the latter is not an 'impression' of the former, where the internal is 'related'. In support of this he claims that a certain very precise physical description, namely that at 2.0003 p.m. the lights changed, and at 2.0003 p.m. his foot began pressing the accelerator, is compatible with four different first-personal reports of the relations of perception and action, and hence with four different third-personal psychological descriptions derived from these. But, on the contrary, it seems to me that there could well be true scientific propositions the conjunction of which with the precise physical statement would be incompatible with any of these psychological descriptions. For we might know that no light-changing could affect an organism in a way mediated by its central nervous system in less than a certain time. Again, we might know that no foot movement that was by ordinary non-scientific criteria counted as action, part of a project, etc., was so unless initiated by nerve impulses starting from the brain (contrast applying stimuli near the foot itself) – and they take time. So if the light change and the start of the movement were within *those* limits objectively simultaneous, then we can surely conclude that any of the reports that O'Shaughnessy cites would be wrong, and (most probably) that the driver in fact anticipated seeing the lights change.

The notion of a *criterial* validity of the first-personal reports in such a case does seem extremely odd. For suppose the physical measurements showed that the start of the foot pressing happened (just a little) before the light change; surely we must then infer that it *couldn't* be the case that he first saw, and then pressed? But what is the essential difference between 'it happened after', 'it didn't happen before', and – the concern of the previous paragraph – 'it didn't happen long enough before'?

Perhaps there are reasons for saying that the internal psychological order is not, in such a case, an 'impression' of a physical order. But this argument to that conclusion, based on the idea that a certain class of psychological reports are not falsifiable by discoveries about the physical order, seems to be mistaken. Perhaps what O'Shaughnessy wants for his position is rather something like this: that while the psychological reports can be falsified by the physical order, they are not to be seen as guesses at it.

(3) On pp. 168-9 O'Shaughnessy gives some arguments about the timing of *decision*. I am not sure what the upshot of these is. He concludes: '... "he decided" need not report successful termination of actively trying to decide, and cannot report an act, extended or extensionless'. He adds that there is no activity of deciding. If an 'activity' is something which takes time, lasts so long, etc., then trying to make up one's mind can presumably be regarded as an activity, as in general 'trying to

x' may be. But not everything I can try to do is an activity in the sense that what follows successful trying is *starting* to x: consider trying to reach an object with a stick, trying to pick up the diamond with the tweezers, trying to get the telescope into focus, trying to recall. In such cases the transition from 'he is trying to x' to 'he has x'd' seems to be instantaneous. But it does not follow that there is no answer to the question of when the agent did any of those things. And in cases in which he did any of those things 'straight-off', without trying, there will be a time at which he did it. I am therefore a bit unclear how O'Shaughnessy's conclusions about the timing of decision are related to his remarks about the activity of trying to decide.

(4) I turn now to a piece of ancillary machinery which O'Shaughnessy uses: his distinction between 'non-autonomous part-events' and autonomous, distinct, constituent events. This is a distinction explicated basically by the consideration of whether there is one common cause or two separate causes; and is illustrated by the examples, on p. 171, of (1) a tennis ball propelled by impact with a racket, and made to waver by air turbulence, as against (2) a tennis ball to which a wavering trajectory is imparted by the character of the tennis stroke; it is of course (2) that is supposed to illustrate non-autonomy.

I cannot think that, at least as supported by such examples, the distinction can bear much weight. Let us start with (1). By the same argument, the air speed and heading of an aircraft, and the velocity of a side wind, constitute two causes, and hence there is a compound character to the resultant track and ground speed. Where the wind is a head or tail wind, we have a compound character for the resultant ground speed. The speed and mass of a satellite together with gravitational forces give a compound character to its orbit. And Galilean analysis of forces must surely, by the same token, give a compound character to the motion in case (2).

Again, in the case of the see-saw, we indeed say that pushing down on one end causes the other end to go up. But pushing down on end a, where that includes the going down of end a, is not of course a causally sufficient condition of end b going up. The see-saw might, for instance, just bend in the middle. We have to add standing conditions of rigidity, etc. And the failure of such conditions might be explained by other incident conditions, as for instance of heat. O'Shaughnessy speaks of causes only in terms of autonomous events (which incidentally imports some circularity into his account). But if the wind-conditions in his first example can count, then not only will the factors which led to the slippery slope with regard to that example, but also various conditions which affect the behaviour of the see-saw.

(5) His highly restricted view of what is involved in a causal account seems to colour O'Shaughnessy's arguments against the putative causal connections between catching sight of X (SX) and acting upon X (AX); and I will end with one remark about this, while recognizing that O'Shaughnessy regards this aspect as less than central to his enterprise.

The general obscurity of what is indeed involved in causality of course provides difficulty for those who plead a causal connection in this and similar psychological matters. But even fairly straightforward considerations about causal explanation shed doubt on O'Shaughnessy's argument, if I have followed it. The argument turns on the point that knowledge of X, KX, is necessary for the beginning and completion of AX. This knowledge is acquired through SX: it 'comes from and with' SX (p.183). 'It follows that SX can contribute to the occurrence of AX only through the mediation of KX. Therefore SX can neither cause nor be a contributory cause of AX.'

This just seems as it stands a *non sequitur*. On the conditions given, SX is of course not the total sufficient condition of AX – how could it be? But it is quite possibly a necessary condition – and what is the argument that it is not a causally necessary condition? Only, it seems, that even contributory causes cannot permit 'action-at-a-distance-in-time in the mind'. But whatever this exactly means, we surely here do not have action at a distance, precisely because of the mediation of KX (if the agent had caught sight of X, and then instantly and totally forgotten all about it, there would indeed be a problem about the connection of SX and AX). It is just not true that 'we must situate all contributory causes at no distance in time from the effect' – very many 'contributory causes' would not be such under this requirement.

193

Index of Names